Lynda Field is a trained specialises in personal author of ten titles, inc *Feel Amazing* and *60 W* to giving seminars and workshops, she writes a column for a major Internet provider, as well as articles for a variety of national magazines. She lives in Essex, UK.

Visit Lynda online at www.lyndafield.com

By the same author:

60 Ways to Change Your Life

60 Ways to Feel Amazing

The Little Book of Woman Power

60 Tips for Self-Esteem

Creating Self-Esteem

60 Ways to Heal Your Life

More than 60 Ways to Make Your Life Amazing

Self-Esteem for Women

The Self-Esteem Workbook

Just Do It Now!

365

INSPIRATIONS FOR A

GREAT
LIFE

LYNDA FIELD

Vermilion
LONDON

5 7 9 10 8 6

First published in 2002 by Vermilion,
an imprint of Ebury Press, Random House,
20 Vauxhall Bridge Road, London SW1V 2SA

Random House Australia (Pty) Limited
20 Alfred Street, Milsons Point, Sydney,
New South Wales 2061, Australia

Random House New Zealand Limited
18 Poland Road, Glenfield, Auckland 10, New Zealand

Random House South Africa (Pty) Limited
Endulini, 5A Jubilee Road, Parktown 2193, South Africa

The Random House Group Limited Reg. No. 954009

Papers used by Rider are natural, recyclable products made from
wood grown in sustainable forests.

Printed and bound by Nørhaven Paperback A/S, Denmark

A CIP catalogue record for this book
is available from the British Library

ISBN 0-09-188757-7

Dedicated to
my granddaughter Alaska,
who is a big inspiration.

Introduction

You are fabulously creative and amazingly talented. You have the power to be all that you want to be and to live your dreams.

But sometimes it's so hard to believe this, isn't it?

365 Inspirations for a Great Life has been designed to uplift and hearten you every day of the year (however bad it gets!)

Start now: make every day count and turn an ordinary life into a great life. Just do it!

With my very best wishes

Lynda Field

For more support and advice visit me at:
www.lyndafield.com

A Happy New You

A Happy New You

A brand new year and a brand new you. Are you full of excitement and hopeful expectancy or does it just feel like more of the same?

Let this be the year that you fill your life with inspiration. You only have to believe in yourself and you can:

- Do what you want to do.
- Be what you want to be.
- Reach your potential.
- Fill your life with joy.

Let the powerful energy of positivity sweep into your life and raise your game. This is the year that you turn an ordinary life into a great life!

Men and Women Are Different

Recent research shows that women are able to feel their emotions and talk about them at the same time (using both sides of the brain). Men can't do this, they can either feel or talk. And so, there is a physical reason why:

> the man in your life finds it hard to talk about his emotions,

or

> the woman in your life is talking and feeling at the same time (and confusing you).

Men cannot express their feelings immediately, but they can on reflection. So talk things over later and not in the heat of disagreement.

Be Full Of It

Have you ever noticed how upbeat people are always so full of everything? They are mad about this, love that and are full of appreciation for all that they have.

And this is the magic key to raising your energy: appreciate your life – the downs as well as the ups.

Sometimes, when we are feeling desperate our heart can be touched by something really simple and we are back on the road to healing.

The world is a wondrous place when we have eyes to see. Look and then look again: you are part of this miracle.

Stop the Rot

When we are feeling low in confidence it's so hard to like anything about ourselves.

If you ever get caught in this negative spiral:

> self-dislike ▸ feelings of powerlessness
> ▸ inability to make decisions ▸ inability to
> act ▸ self-dislike

there is a way to stop the rot!

- Remember a time when you were confident and upbeat.

- Recreate the feelings again.

- Imagine that you are feeling good about yourself again – and before you know it you are!

Stay with this feeling.

Cherish Your Valuables

When it comes right down to it, we discover that the things we value most in our lives are not our material goods. Our gold watch is nice, that designer suit is a wonderful fit, the new car is very swish ... but these things have no real meaning in themselves.

Sometimes it takes a while for us to recognise the most valued things in our life. Ask yourself:

- What are my real valuables?
- What brings meaning and purpose to my life?
- What is most important to me?
- Who are the people who are most important to me?

A Victim No More!

Do you ever feel taken for granted, overworked, unappreciated, misunderstood and resentful?

Think about a particular situation where you are feeling victimised and ask yourself these questions:

- Who is treating me badly?

- Why am I letting them do this to me?

- What do I need to do to change this behaviour?

You might have to stand up for yourself. Perhaps you need to say 'no' to someone. You may even need to walk away from the whole situation. Do whatever it takes. You are not a victim unless you choose to be!

Search For the Hero

You have untapped potential and unrealised strengths: you can become the person you most want to be!

- Make a list of your personal heroes and heroines.
- Next to their names write exactly why you admire them.
- Reflect on those qualities that you so admire in others.

If you can recognise certain strengths and abilities in others then you must be aware of the capacity for these same abilities in yourself (or you would never have recognised them in other people).

Search for the hero inside yourself and use your own amazing gifts to realise your incredible potential.

Get Noticed

You will never get that promotion, job with a large salary, stunning and recognisable success, or whatever it is that you most desire if you don't step forward and get yourself noticed for the right things.

- Be seen by people who can help you, and get networking.

- Be in the right place at the right time.

- Make sure your self-image is positive and assured; walk tall and you will look and feel more confident.

- Fake it until you make it – which means that you act assertively even if you don't feel it.

Shrinking violets never win the big prizes.

Clean Your Aura

- Sit quietly and relax.

- Become aware of your aura – this is the energy which surrounds your physical body.

- In your mind's eye imagine a halo of light around your body. Visualise this as an unbroken line of light surrounding you.

- Send a beam of cleansing white line around the contour of your aura. Imagine this light acting like a vacuum cleaner sucking out any negativity.

- When your aura is sparkling and clean open your eyes.

When your auric energy is shining you will shine too!

On a Bad Hair Day

Whenever you find yourself preoccupied with minutiae (sagging body parts, a broken nail, a bad hair day) lift yourself up and take a larger perspective. Ask yourself the following questions:

- Who are the people you most love in the world?
- What quality do you most admire in yourself?
- What would you love to accomplish?
- Are you afraid to take chances?
- Do you believe in yourself?
- What is the most amazing thing you have ever done?
- What holds you back?

The quality of your life is more important than the way you look!

Tips for Success at Work

- It's unusual for someone to just 'know' their true vocation from the start. It takes most of us some time to discover where our skills lie, so be patient and keep working towards your goals.

- Take your spirituality to the workplace. Use your intuitive awareness and natural empathy and kindness at work and you will be amazed by the way that others respond. Show them that their contribution is important.

- Make positive affirmations for your success ('I can do this') and visualise its reality (see your success in your mind's eye).

Oh All Right Then

It can sometimes be difficult to distinguish the difference between being a good friend / neighbour / partner / workmate, etc. and being a victim.

When are you operating from the goodness of your heart and when is it just a case of you being unable to say 'no'? Ah, such a little word, but one that many of us will do almost anything to avoid saying. Consider the following:

- Can you remember the last time you agreed to do something that you didn't want to do?
- How did you feel as you were being asked?
- How did you act?
- Why didn't you say 'no'?
- Next time say it!

Your Character Test

Are you a positive or negative person (or a bit of both)?

Personality traits to look out for:

- Fear of rejection (negative)
- Good sense of humour, can laugh at self (positive)
- Worried about not being liked (negative)
- Genuinely likes people and shows interest in them (positive)
- Has to have the last word, must be right (negative)
- Can say sorry when necessary (positive)
- Self-centred (negative)
- Good listener (positive)
- Low self-esteem (negative)

Accentuate the positive, always!

Feeling Empowered at Work

Ways to keep assertive in the workplace:

- Take advantage of your natural intuitive abilities – be guided by your instincts.

- Never demean yourself; keep positive and confident about your abilities.

- Use the tools of negotiation to get what you want; for example, use a positive approach such as 'How can we come to some agreement?'

- Don't ever let yourself be forced into making a decision; take time to think if you need to.

- Be a good listener – this is one of the most effective communication tools. Others will feel valued and you will hear everything you need to hear.

The Music of the Spheres

When you feel trapped in the whirlwind of your life, STOP! Try this simple yet wonderful meditation technique.

Relax and close your eyes. Now tune in to any sound that you can hear in your head.

Home in on it until it is the main sound in your mind. Let all other sounds and thoughts pass by.

As you let this sound fill your consciousness you will ultimately merge with it until you can no longer hear it.

Listen for as long as you feel comfortable and enjoy what is called 'the music of the spheres'.

Young at Heart

We can enjoy the freedom of adulthood and the pleasures of childhood if we remain young at heart.

Fun people can be any age: staying young is an attitude and it has nothing to do with how old we are.

Get in touch with some childhood memories which link you to your past.

These may be rekindled by any sense experience: the touch of velvet, the taste of an aniseed ball, the smell of the sea, the sound of a church bell, a ride on a carousel ...

Recreate some childhood experiences and stay forever young at heart.

There Are No Obstacles in Your Way!

Hard to believe but true: we create our own limitations. That glass ceiling is an illusion that you have created out of fear and self-doubt. And the place where you sit, underneath this ceiling, is your illusory comfort zone.

I know, we all crave the comfort of security and familiarity but we can't stay in the same place forever – it's like living in an open prison! We often cling to what we know because we are afraid to make changes: what if we fail ... make mistakes ... people laugh at us ...? Forget your fear and be what you want to be!

You Are Good Enough

Have you ever been in that no-win situation where even your best is not enough for you, when the only way to feel in control is to be perfect, even when you know that perfectionism is unattainable?

There's a fine line between the wonderful expansiveness that comes as we reach for our potential, and the unbearable limitation of never ever feeling quite good enough. A desire to do well can become an addiction; we can even start beating ourselves up for not being positive enough!

Consider this: you are good enough just the way you are.

Yes, it's true!

— 19 —

How to Stop Arguing

When things are getting you down, do you often take it out on our nearest and dearest?

Take these four steps:

1 Recognise your negative state of mind and decide to step out from this downward spiral.

2 Hit your 'stop button'. Imagine a button lit up in red with 'STOP' on it. This imaginary button will stop your emotional whirl for a moment.

3 Identify your immediate needs (to talk / to spend time alone / to receive tea and sympathy).

4 Calmly express your needs so that your loved ones can give you the exact response you need.

Look Out for Others

Everyone struggles with self-doubt at different times in their lives, so look around and see who could do with your support at the moment. You can make such a difference to the way that someone is feeling.

Try one or all of the following:

- Listen well – show that you care.

- Demonstrate your appreciation in a tangible way.

- Send a letter or a card – this can mean so much.

- Plan an outing; just meeting for a drink can make all the difference.

- Keep in touch, even when the bad patch has passed.

The Good News About You

It's time to drop those negative thoughts about yourself, they are only getting in your way. Never mind whatever it is you think you can't do; let's look at your assets.

Complete the following:

- My best asset is my ....
- I feel confident when ....
- The best thing about my personality is
  ....
- The thing I like best about my body is ....
- The most amazing thing I have ever done is
  ....
- I feel powerful when ....

Assess your answers and reflect on their meaning. Focus on the good news about yourself. You have everything going for you!

Beyond Your Comfort Zone

If you feel like you are in a rut, it's time to expand your comfort zone (otherwise known as changing your habits!)

- What did you love to do ten years ago that you don't do now?

- Which of these things would you like to do again?

- Ask yourself why you have stopped doing these things.

- Go back another ten years and repeat this exercise.

- Go back as far as you can.

- Now choose one thing from your list and DO IT.

- How do you feel? Choose another one and another one ...

Know Yourself

Your stability, endurance and integrity depend on your inner resources, and the quality of your life will reflect them.

Learn to know yourself by developing a strong and confident connection with your inner strengths.

- Always face facts – denial leads to pain.
- Speak your truth even if others find it difficult to hear.
- Be courageous and move forward, even if it feels uncomfortable.
- Never compare yourself with others.
- Take full responsibility for your actions.
- Show compassion.

Become the person you would most like to spend your life with!

Believe in Yourself

'If you believe that you can do a thing, or if you believe you cannot, in either case you are right.'

(Henry Ford)

And there you have it in a nutshell. You are what you believe you are and you will become whatever you expect to become – the choice is yours! If you always take passive, submissive and receptive roles and never expect the best for yourself, then your life will always feel like a B movie.

Increase your self-expectations – you really can do more, be more and create more. Trust your judgement and believe in yourself.

Seek Abundance

- Go out and experience the abundance of the universe.

- Look at the oceans, look at the sky, look at the kindness of the human heart.

- Open a tomato and see how many seeds are inside.

- Nature did not intend us either to go short of tomatoes or not to share our gifts.

The more you seek abundance and prosperity the more it will enter your life, and so it will enter the lives of others. What goes around comes around!

A Winning Mentality

Sports psychology has demonstrated that winning has as much to do with mental strength as ability: in other words, a positive attitude leads to success.

At least 70 per cent of our daily thoughts are negative (how much more on a bad day?) Negativity is a major obstacle to success, so we need to develop a good positive attitude in order to create winning situations in our everyday lives.

Start the day on a positive note.

- When you open your eyes be glad for the day.
- Expect the best.
- Choose positivity over negativity every time.

Your Spiritual Self

Points to remember:

- Because you are human you are naturally spirituall.

- Your spirituality gives you your love of life.

- Connecting with your spirituality does not involve a journey into a strange and unknown world, but a reconnection with an experience that you have known all along.

- When you open to your spiritual dimension you open your life to new meaning and purpose.

- The keys to awareness are within you: trust your intuitive voice.

- Love is all you need.

Embrace your spiritual self and amazing things will begin to happen.

Calling All Wonder Women

Women are very good at doing three things at once (and the rest), and this wonderful skill can often lead us into dissatisfaction.

We finish a great project, but we have so many other plans, so little time and so much still to do!

No, we can't stop because the goalposts have moved and we are still running to keep up with ourselves.

If you have ever felt like this, pause for a moment and just take some space for yourself.

Yes, take a five-minute break from the whirlwind of your life and be here now, in this moment, taking this one breath.

Ways to Be Happy at Work

1 Stop using the 'stress' label. If work life is troublesome understand the difficulties and then try to resolve them.

2 Be specific about the problems; it then becomes easier to find solutions.

3 Discuss your situation with a trusted friend.

4 Don't moan or gossip, this path leads to a negative place.

5 Express your needs assertively.

6 Don't let yourself be victimised by others. Whenever you act like a victim, others will treat you like one.

7 Think of your work problems as challenges that you can overcome.

8 Use a creative approach to problem-solving.

9 Keep positive and confident and people will treat you with respect.

Heal Your Life

Make any of these affirmations as often as you can.
Write them, say them, sing them. Surround yourself with
healing consciousness and feel your energy respond.

I deserve vibrant health.

I love my body.

I can heal myself.

I listen and respond to my body's messages.

I create harmony and balance within my body.

The universal life-force flows easily through me.

I trust my inner messages.

It is safe to be well.

I am ready to be well now.

I love and value myself.

In Balance

We are built for mental, physical, emotional and spiritual activity. Creativity and high confidence levels depend upon the balance of these activities. If you are feeling less than your best, check to see if you are in balance by answering the following questions:

- How much mental activity have I had today?
- How much physical activity have I had today?
- How long have I been in touch with my emotions today?
- How much spiritual activity have I had today?

Discover where the imbalance lies and then look through this book to find ways to re-establish a balance in your life.

Choose to Be Positive

You wake up feeling not so brilliant. There are two options you can take.

1 You drag yourself to work moaning all the way. You are not looking your best (grumpy face, slumping body posture), which makes you feel even worse. You look so miserable that people keep away from you. And down you go even further.

2 You decide to make this a positive day (however bad you feel). You smile (increases your endorphin levels and makes you feel better after 10 seconds!) Others are keen to communicate with you (you look receptive). Your mood is improving as you enter the positive cycle. This day can only get better and better!

— 2 —

Loving Yourself

Did you know that loving yourself opens you up to receiving all the great things in life? Self-appreciation does not mean that you are egotistical and selfish, it just means that you can value your human beingness.

By using positive and loving affirmations and visualisations you can create new and powerful energy. Try this:

- Look into a mirror and say to yourself, 'I love and appreciate you.'

- Close your eyes and see yourself looking calm and centred.

- Remind yourself at all times that you are an amazing and lovable person, because you are!

Be Popular

Become the friend that you would most like to have. If you would like to be popular and attract new people into your circle, then use the following skills.

- Extend your interests – and your personal network will develop.

- Empathise with others and show them that you understand.

- Listen well. Give people your undivided attention and they will feel valued and respected.

- Develop your ability to make small-talk; find out what interests the other person. People feel more able to relax when the tone is light-hearted.

As you become recognised as a person who is non-threatening and supportive, you will attract new relationships.

Zap Up Your Sex Life

- Get flirty with your partner.

- Focus your attention on your sex life; let it become your main thing. If it's losing its appeal then talk about it, to each other.

- Think about sex (this works like a dream!)

- Remember what first attracted you to your partner; recreate that romance and intimacy.

- Spend time alone together. Turn off the TV, stop talking about domestic issues and enjoy being with each other.

- Laugh together – humour is such a great turn on!

- Plan a special date together to celebrate how much you mean to each other.

Rainbow Healing

- Imagine a fountain of cascading rainbow light. All the colours of the spectrum are here in their brilliant hues.

- Now think of someone who needs support at this time.

- Visualise them stepping into the fountain and being immersed in the colours.

- They will absorb the colours they need.

You don't need to do anything else. Know that they are being assisted at the very highest energy level. See the person emerge looking and feeling good.

Your strong intention to help creates the healing energy.

Whose Life Is This?

How many times do we really desire to make a change in our lives but we feel too afraid to take that risky next step?

What would you like to change?

What exactly are the risks involved?

Well, daring to change might involve the following risks:

- Failure
- Rejection
- Being ridiculed
- People not liking you any more

How much do these things matter to you? Whose life is this anyway?

Meet Your Happy Self

Relax and close your eyes.

- Count backwards from 100 as you imagine yourself descending a beautiful white marble staircase.

- Each time you count, you take another step down.

- You see someone coming up the steps to meet you; it's you, and you are looking very happy.

- Meet your happy self on the stairs and feel her / his energy and enthusiasm.

- Look carefully at this part of you. Notice and absorb all its positive characteristics.

- Embrace your happy self and feel your oneness as you merge.

Skip lightly back up the steps feeling happy and fantastic!

Finish It!

How many of your inspirations are lying half finished in a carrier bag somewhere in your house? How many DIY disasters lurk in dark corners? We all have half-completed jobs (time ran out, inspiration ran out, skill levels couldn't quite make it ...) and we keep thinking that we ought to finish them.

These unfinished projects are wind-ups – they stop new inspiration coming through. Throw them out and forget all about them or finish them!

- List your unfinished jobs
- Which ones can be trashed?
- Bin these.
- Choose one of the rest and finish it!

Be ready for new inspirations.

Tips for Relaxation

1 Don't bring work home.

2 Create a real weekend off.

3 Turn off your mobile.

4 Remember that your mind, body and soul need to relax.

5 Turn off the TV.

6 Take out your diary and schedule some relaxation time.

7 Treat yourself to a massage.

8 Consciously slow down your breathing – you will feel more tranquil.

9 Don't fill every moment of your waking day; let there be some spaces where you can stand and stare and daydream.

10 Consider why you are called a human being and not a human doing – learn to let yourself be.

What do You Love to Do?

You bring your own unique set of skills and strengths to the planet, and until you discover and use these amazing abilities you will feel dissatisfied and discontented.

If you are struggling to become the person you most want to be, just look deep within yourself to find what really inspires and motivates you. What do you absolutely love to do? What turns you on?

Are you demonstrating this passion in your life's work? If not, then why not?

Too Busy to Be Happy

Do you ever have time to stand and stare? I know there's a lot to be done, but the truth is that the world won't stop just because you have! When you get so busy that you don't have time to be happy, it's time to reassess.

Why you might be afraid to stop:

1 Fear of change

2 Desire to be perfect

3 Too anxious to delegate

4 Unrealistic self-expectations

5 Fear of intimacy

6 Needing to be needed

7 Believing that life can't be fun

Your life is a wonderful gift. Take time to love and appreciate it.

Letting Joy into Your Life

Joy is not the result of something happening to you, although it may seem like it. No, joy is a feeling that lies inside you; let yourself feel it.

You always have a choice in life: are you going to take the path of joy or the path of struggle?

- Just for today try the joyful path.

- Suspend your cynicism and negative expectations and look for joy in every encounter.

- When people are unkind, thoughtless and complaining, just recognise that they are taking the path of struggle and you are choosing to have a different experience.

Being a Busy Bee

The 24-hour 21st-century society means that we can all be on the go all day and all night. But even busy bees stop buzzing after the sun has set!

Not so very long ago, before electric lighting, people were forced to live at a slower pace and were more in tune with their own natural rhythms and the cycles of the seasons. But now our natural working day does not necessarily start at dawn and end at dusk, it can go on and on until we decide to stop – and some of us don't know when to stop.

Stop buzzing and relax!

Every Exit Is an Entry

Every cloud has a silver lining; there is a meaning and a purpose to everything that happens to you.

When you are facing a problem ask yourself the following questions:

- How did this happen?

- How can I view this situation differently?

- In what way can this loss work for me?

- What can I learn about myself here?

- What is there that is positive in this situation?

- What is the first step I need to take so that I can bounce back quickly?

As one door closes another opens. Look for the newly opening door; look for the silver lining.

Never Mind the Weather

Everyone goes on about the weather – it's too hot, too cold, too windy, too wet, too dry, lovely now but it will never last, too good for the time of the year ...

Why would we want to become victims of the weather when we are working so hard to be positive and assertive?

If you have ever been upset about the temperature, the rain, the fog, the sun ... consider this:

We cannot change the weather.

Never allow yourself to be victimised by something that you cannot change – this is a classic case of self-victimisation. Never mind the weather, get out and enjoy your life.

You Don't Always Have to Be Right

As soon as you stop always trying to be right you will discover how delightfully relaxing this position is. Why do you need to bother to defend your beliefs and thoughts (unless you have a job as a politician!)? Arguing with others just gives you a headache and makes everyone uptight. Try this:

- Let others have their say even if you don't agree with them.
- Let others have their say especially if you don't agree with them.
- Stop defending your position (you don't need to).

Try this and notice how the atmosphere lightens up!

Life's Gifts

The real gifts of life cannot be bought from anywhere. In fact they often come disguised as difficulties, obstacles and problems, which we would rather avoid.

But when we rise to the challenges of life we find inside ourselves such amazing strengths: hope; endurance; patience; wisdom; optimism ...

The Chinese symbol for 'crisis' is the same as the one for 'opportunity'. But you may have to look carefully at your challenges to find the hidden gifts they bring.

Look for such things as:

- Inner strength
- A greater sense of purpose and meaning
- Increased resilience

You can overcome anything.

Create New Boundaries

Sometimes everyone seems to need us, don't they? Little wonder that we often feel like shouting, 'What about me?' Shout it and then take some action.

The next time someone asks you for a favour do the following:

- Don't automatically agree to do it.

- Assess your real feelings. If you know that saying 'yes' will cause you to feel fear, anger, resentment, low self-esteem or even just confusion, then it's time to create a new boundary line.

- Say to yourself, 'I will go this far and no further.'

- Remember that you can be a good friend / parent / partner / workmate and still say 'no'.

Love Your Enemies

Anger and hatred do nothing to improve our mood whereas forgiveness always makes us feel fantastic (the gifts it brings are the greatest we can receive). Try this:

- Make a list of all the people you can't stand.

- Next time you meet one of them imagine that this is their last day on earth; you will never see them again.

- Now take this opportunity to clean up this relationship – take that step towards reconciliation (you will be amazed by the effect).

Forgiveness is hard but possible, and if you truly intend to change your poor relationships you will!

Appreciating Others

Make a list of the people you appreciate. For example:

*I appreciate my best friend because she is always
full of fun and laughter.*

*I appreciate my mother, who is determined to
overcome her physical difficulties.*

*I appreciate my partner, who is always there for
me, even when I am in a bad mood.*

*I appreciate my daughter, who always manages to
keep optimistic even when the going gets rough.*

*I appreciate my team at work because they always
manage to get the job done well.*

Your list of wonderful people will make you smile and
uplift your heart.

Appreciation is the key to happiness. Appreciate this!

Accentuate the Positive

Thoughts are like powerful magnets: they attract matching energy patterns. This means that whatever we focus our attention on will grow.

Think negatively and you will quickly spiral into depression (negativity just attracts more of the same). Replace your negatives with positives.

- If you feel angry, think the biggest loving thought that you can (positive energy is always more powerful than negative energy).

- If you feel stressed, just stop for a moment and visualise a beautiful, tranquil scene.

- If you feel like a loser, remind yourself that everything you do is a success.

Nine Important Things

Know these things and your life will transform:

- Dreams can come true – believe in them.
- How to say what you mean – life will be a breeze.
- Expect the best – you get what you expect.
- Forgiveness creates happiness – decide to let go.
- How to say no – you will stop being a victim.
- Everything changes – bad times will pass.
- How to accept a compliment – smile and say thanks.
- Persistence pays – don't take no for an answer.
- How to smile dazzlingly – it will light up your life.

— 23 —

Trust Your Intuition

Are you feeling immobilised? Do you need a fresh take on your life?

Try this:

- Think of a difficult situation that needs a new creative response (your old way of handling it just isn't working).
- Relax, close your eyes and ask your intuition to help you to resolve your problem.
- Repeat this process over the next few days.
- Be prepared to receive new insights.
- Trust this new information.
- Act on it!

Your intuition is infinitely knowledgeable, creative and resourceful; use this power to add deeper meaning to life.

Believe in Miracles

Miracles are love in action. Their defining feature is that they will only happen to us if we believe in them.

Use your creative energy to attract a miracle.

- Expect a miracle for a week.

- Suspend all disbelief; fear of disappointment can stand in your way forever.

- Wholeheartedly believe that a miracle will happen, and keep trusting.

- The miracle may not take the form that you were expecting.

- But be assured, something amazing will happen.

Belief is the strongest magic of all.

Make Room For the New

Clear out the clutter in your life and you will be amazed at the effect this has on you.

- Throw out all old unfinished projects.
- Send all those clothes (that you are waiting to fit into) to the charity shop.
- Tackle that cupboard where the contents fall on the floor whenever you open the door.

Start with these simple clearance tasks and as you make space and transform your environment you will begin to clear your mind and feel a greater sense of control and purpose.

Let this burst of confidence inspire new action.

You Are Worth It

Radiate self-esteem and you will look and feel sensational.

- Fight your natural inclination to dislike yourself, and start to appreciate your unique and special look.

- Don't compare yourself with glossy media images, you will always be disappointed.

- You are so much more than your dress size, always remember this.

- The most exciting and attractive woman is the one who radiates self-esteem; she knows her true worth.

- Say the following mantra to yourself: 'I am perfect just the way I am.'

- Be body confident. Use assertive body language and show that you respect yourself.

You Are a Walking Miracle

Yes, truly you are. I know, you feel too fat / too thin / not successful enough / not clever enough ... but you really are good enough, just the way you are!

Forget your hang-ups and take a long slow look around you. There is just so much to appreciate and give thanks for, and appreciation makes you feel fabulous, there is no doubt.

I want you to try this, just for today. Today your mantra is, 'I appreciate my life.' Say this throughout the day and whenever you remember give thanks and count your blessings. Notice the difference in your day.

Overcoming Setbacks

We are always having to face difficult situations where things don't go the way we want them to – life's like that!

Try the following to help you to overcome your obstacles:

- Whenever you feel rejected, fed up, unloved or out of control recognise your feelings and then move on.

- Remember that no one has a clear path through life. Keep upbeat.

- Ask yourself how important this incident is in the grand scheme of your life.

- Respect the way you deal with a difficult situation.

- Change your attitude (for example, if they won't employ you that's their loss; if your relationship has ended, maybe you are better off single).

Be Forgiving

Forgiveness is all about letting go: if you can't forgive someone, your angry thoughts will connect you with them forever.

Is there someone you find it difficult to forgive? If so, ask yourself what you are gaining from not forgiving this person. Then take the following steps:

- Examine exactly what hurt you and why.
- Express this is in an appropriate way.
- Forgive, let go and set yourself free.

If this feels just too hard, then try visualising yourself forgiving the person. This will have a powerful effect on your relationship with them. Hard to believe? Try it and see for yourself.

Does It Really Matter

Whenever you feel yourself getting tense or upset about something, ask yourself this important question, 'Does it really matter?'

If it does, then be sure to express your feelings to the right person. However, very often we allow ourselves to become worked up about something that really doesn't matter, and then our irritation can quickly lead into a bad mood.

When we feel low the minor details in life can become blown up out of all proportion. So next time you are getting annoyed over a small issue, ask yourself if it matters, and if it doesn't, just let go and move on.

Live It to the Limit

Who knows how long our lifespan will be? But one thing is for sure: we are all leaving the planet eventually. The only life we know we have for a certainty is this one, and the only moment we have for sure is this moment. So live it to the limit! This doesn't mean behaving recklessly and crazily, rather it means the opposite:

- Appreciate each moment.
- Be glad to be alive.
- Make every communication count.
- Love this precious gift of your life.
- Don't put off the important things.
- Tell others how much they mean to you (why are you waiting to do this?)

Emotional Burnout

We all have times when everything gets too much and we become emotionally drained.

If you are feeling exhausted, and there is no medical reason for your condition, then it's time to stop and evaluate your situation.

Check your emotional state.

- Are you going through an emotional crisis?
- Have you taken on too many responsibilities?
- Are you carrying an emotional burden?
- Do you feel as if there is nowhere to turn?
- Are you looking after yourself (good nutrition, enough exercise, enough sleep)?
- Do you feel empty inside?

If you need help, ask for it. Put yourself first right now.

Don't Sit on Your Anger

We are so afraid of our anger and go to great lengths to cover it up. But anger is a natural emotion and like all our feelings it needs to be acknowledged and expressed in some way. Supressed anger can lead to depression and physical illness.

The next time you feel angry do the following:

1 Admit your feelings.

2 Work out why you are angry.

3 Find some form of immediate release
   (exercise, pillow bashing, silent screaming ...)

4 Express your feelings to a trusted friend.

5 If something needs to be said to someone,
   then go ahead and say it!

Forgive Your Parents

You may have recognised some of your own negative behaviours in your parents. But remember, we can only teach and pass on what we know, and that is what they did.

We can never let go of our own negativity and replace it with positivity if we are still blaming our parents for whatever it is we think they have 'done' to us. Start to forgive your parents and you will feel like a new person.

Don't let blame hold you back. Step out of your child-hood shoes; you are a responsible grown-up now. And remember, your parents had parents too.

Connect from Your Heart

When we are feeling full of love we automatically open up our heart. When we communicate from this energy centre we are able to connect at the highest possible level. As love flows out and love flows in we are inter-acting with each other in the most meaningful way we can.

- Visualise a big golden sunflower in the middle of your chest.
- Each time you communicate with another person, see their sunflower.

An amazing thing happens; you will find that others will respond with much more than their usual warmth.

Have a giant sunflower day and feel the difference.

Twist and Shout

Let go of pent-up emotion with this brilliant and funny exercise:

1 Stand tall, feet shoulder width apart.

2 Swing your body, neck and head, as one unit, first to one side and then to the other.

3 As your body twists from side to side let your arms swing loosely and freely so that they wrap around you at your shoulders, your head following your body as you swing.

4 As you are swinging from right to left and back again, shout 'You can't make me!' as loudly as possible.

5 Have fun doing this. Try shouting 'No I won't' or 'I don't care'.

Your Darkest Hour

When we are going through a personal crisis we will not feel inclined to take helpful advice on how to 'feel better'. Quick self-help tips are not the answer here.

We need to feel our feelings, to experience our pain fully before we can let it go and move on. Remember this when others are in the depths of despair, and remember this when you too are floundering in the dark.

The darkest hour is truly just before the dawn. Know this to be true and never give up on the miraculous process of life.

Act on Your Instincts

Your intuition speaks with a voice that just 'knows' something to be right or true, even if there is absolutely no logical reason why you should think so.

We often find it hard to trust our hunches and flashes of insight because we have been taught to reason things out rationally. But, as you know, our rational mind can't always provide the answers!

- Your intuition works at the highest creative level.

- It can answer all your needs.

- You must trust it and act upon it.

- The more you do this, the clearer its voice becomes.

Step into Your Future

This very powerful visualisation will draw the next step of your dream into your life.

- Relax and close your eyes.

- Imagine your life's work as a symbol.

- See yourself holding your symbol close to your body.

- Feel the energy of this symbol as you absorb its essence.

- Imagine a hill ahead of you.

- Carry your symbol to the top of the hill. There you will see an arched gateway. This is the gateway to your future.

- Step through the gateway, throw your symbol high in the air and watch it fly out into the world that is your future.

Welcoming Change

We can long for change but fear it at the same time. Whatever you want to change – career, partner, lifestyle, the colour of your hair – you may find it hard to get started. Change may feel like a risky business (what if I haven't got what it takes or people laugh at me for trying something new ...?)

But let's get real, the biggest risks come when you are too afraid to change: a life of unachieved potential is a very risky path to take.

Don't live with disappointment.

Why are you waiting? Just do whatever it takes, right now!

The Wow Factor

What is it that makes some women appear so glamorous and fascinating? What is that indefinable ingredient that has men stopping in their tracks? No, it's not that new eye shadow or expensive designer dress or even a wrinkle-free face; it's something that glows from within and is vibrant, energetic, and very alive and exciting.

The most attractive woman in the room is not necessarily the youngest or the one with the perfect figure or the most beautiful skin. She is the one who exudes inner confidence and self-awareness. Glamour comes from within.

Beating Stress

The next time you think you are suffering from stress do
the following:

- Recognise that you are only experiencing a
  feeling of being unable to cope.

- Look at your situation and ask yourself why you
  can't cope.

- Ask yourself if you can do anything to resolve
  the situation?

- If you can't, then accept this and let go of the
  worry.

- If you can, then make an action plan.

- Make a list of the practical steps you need to
  take.

- Then ACT!

- Take each step as it comes and work your way
  through this dilemma.

Love Relationship Test

- Have your love relationships ever caused you emotional pain?

- If yes, then can you describe the situation and your feelings?

- Did you let these situations repeat?

- If yes, why did you let this happen?

- Are you in a love relationship now which is causing you emotional pain?

- Do you ever find yourself making excuses for your man / woman?

- Why do you feel that you have to do this?

- Does he / she find it difficult to express emotions?

- Are you waiting for him / her to change?

What do your answers reveal about you and your lover?

Relax and Be Yourself

Life gets very hectic, and we are all busy running about doing this, that and the other.

This busyness can feel great when it is giving us direction, meaning and purpose. But activity alone can easily become meaningless and pointless. Excessive 'doing' can lead to exhaustion and boredom. Do you ever feel like this?

To lead a balanced and happy life we need to be able to step off the treadmill when the 'doing' gets too much. We need time to just 'be'.

- Learn to relax.
- Stop 'doing'.
- Just be yourself.

Your stress levels will drop and life will look good again.

Be Assertive on the Phone

If you feel ill at ease using the phone or you have a particularly difficult call to make, do it standing up. Although you can't see the person you are calling, you will feel at a physical and psychological advantage.

Smile into the phone. Sounds crazy? When you smile, you sound more confident and assertive, and people treat you with more respect. Smiling also increases your feelings of well-being, so maybe that phone call will not be as intimidating an experience as you expect.

We Are All Connected

Modern physics confirms what spiritual traditions have always taught: our physical universe is made of energy and all forms of energy are interrelated and affect each other.

This means that your contribution does make a difference: your energy affects everyone else's energy. In just the same way that trees and plants are connected (they all have their roots anchored in the earth), we humans are also connected.

Every time you feel uplifted your positive energy bounces onto other people and off them onto others. Moods are contagious because at a very basic level we are all connected. Always remember this!

The Most Powerful Thought

Consider this:

If you think you can, you can, and if you think you can't, you can't. You will always prove yourself right; you are always creating a self-fulfilling prophecy.

Whenever you are feeling knee-deep in negativity remember this: the biggest most powerful thought is always the positive one; it will sweep all else away with its intention, focus and determination. Never underestimate the power of positivity; it will always empower and uplift you. Always choose to think the biggest thought.

Keep believing in life and keep believing in yourself.

Be Assertive at Work

Answer the following:

- Do you ever feel victimised at work?

- Are you ever discriminated against?

- Are you unhappy at work?

If you answered 'yes' to any of these questions, then it's time to take stock.

- Can you say 'no'?

- Are you able to express your needs clearly?

- Are you prepared to take responsibility for yourself, for your actions and decisions?

If there really is nothing you can do to change your situation at work, you can always leave. However, amazing things start to happen to us when we stop acting like a victim and decide to take control of our lives.

Unconditional Love

Do you ever feel that you could be more loving towards a person if only they would change or behave in a different way?

Conditional love depends upon each person keeping their side in an emotional deal (usually unspoken), whereas unconditional love opens the hearts of the giver and receiver.

Learn to love without conditions; love people just the way that they are. If someone is irritating you, say to yourself, 'I love you just the way you are.'

Loving unconditionally is not easy, but it gets easier the more you practise. This way of loving brings forgiveness and peace.

Make This a Special Day

With hopefulness and an optimistic spring in your step you have the power to change a lot of negative energy into positive energy. Make this a special day and make the following affirmations:

Today I will smile whenever I remember to.

Today I will believe in myself 100 per cent.

Today I will only encourage, I will not criticise.

Today I will love my life.

Today I will keep positive.

Today I will forgive myself.

Today I will perform a secret act of kindness.

Today I will be compassionate.

Why not try it again tomorrow?

Smile, Smile, Smile

Yesterday, deep in serious contemplation on the early morning train, I caught the eye of a young woman who gave me a fabulous smile. And my whole day changed from grey to dazzling. I felt my energy lift and I started smiling at everyone I met. What a difference a smile makes!

It is so much easier to rise to your challenges when you are feeling upbeat and positive. Keep things in perspective and remember to give yourself (and everyone else) a lift.

Smile and the world smiles with you.

Away to the Beach

Even those people who are always brimming with confidence have to deal with a well-developed Inner Critic.

Our Inner Critic is that part of us that is always telling us off, saying that we are not good enough / clever enough / thin enough, etc.

Why not send your Inner Critic on holiday?

Imagine him / her sitting on a palm-fringed beach, sipping a cool drink, happy and relaxed and well away from you. Next time you start bringing yourself down, just send your Inner Critic on holiday again by repeating this visualisation.

Leave the Rat Race

If the pace is getting you down, it's time to reassess your direction.

Perhaps you need to downsize in some way. You might decide to take a lower paid job because it feels more worthwhile, or you may move to the country and just slow down.

If you are seriously considering a change of direction, make the following assessment of your situation:

- How can I pay the mortgage / rent?
- How can I follow my mission (vocation)?
- How can I get the balance right (make enough money and still be happy)?

Change is always possible – others have gone before!

Look for More

Try this technique to help you to reach a state of alert and enhanced awareness. See this wonderful world through a softer lens and you will make many new discoveries.

- Become aware of the focus of your vision. How far can you see around you?

- Now stop and consciously expand your awareness – you will feel your focus 'softening' as you do this.

Try looking 'softly' and more expansively whenever you remember. Look for more and you will experience more. Keep practising this!

Love Handles and Flabby Bits

Can you answer these questions:

- Why do so many high-profile women lose about a quarter of their body weight when they hit the big time?

- Why on earth should fame and success contribute to huge weight losses?

- Do you know why love handles and other flabby bits are taboo subjects when nearly everyone wobbles in at least one area of their body?

The answers lie in that crazy, glossy media-hyped world where we can never have a body that is 'good enough'.

Step out of the craziness. Your body is perfect just the way that it is!

Saying No

One simple way to improve the quality of your life is to learn to say 'no'.

Four easy ways to say 'no'

1 Practise saying 'no' while looking in a mirror; get used to saying it out loud.

2 Think of someone you would like to be able to stand up to. Visualise yourself saying 'no' to this person.

3 Decide to let go of guilt and just go for it.

4 Imagine how good you will feel after you have done it.

Split-up and Fed-up?

It's amazing how low we can feel at the end of an important relationship, even if we decided to end it. We may feel unattractive and unloved; low in self-esteem; mistrustful of men (or women); incapable of making decisions; lonely ... and many other mixed emotions. If you are in this situation there is one vitally important thing to remember:

Every one of your relationships is a reflection of the relationship you are having with yourself.

So turn your attention on yourself and forget about relationships until you are feeling more confident and centred.

Choose to Be Glad

You can choose your view of the world:

- Your cup can be half empty or half full.

- You can make things happen or have things happen to you.

- You can think worrying thoughts every waking moment of your day or you can fill your mind with more pleasant things.

Yes, you really do have this choice. Of course it's no good just sticking your head in the sand and pretending your problems will go away; if things need tackling then sort them out. Act rather than worry.

Scientists say that excessive worrying affects more than two million people in the UK. Don't be one of them!

The Man You Want

Fed up with picking up his socks and putting down the toilet seat? Is there a grimy ring around the bath and a pile of towels on the bathroom floor?

If you answer yes to any of these questions then I have to tell you that the fault is all yours.

Why let men go on and on puzzling about what women really want when we can clearly tell them?

We want kind, caring partners who listen to our needs and know how to clean the toilet! Teach the man in your life how to become the man you most want him to be (balanced, sensitive and housework-friendly).

Do Whatever Turns You On

It is not necessary to take mood-altering drugs in order to improve the way we feel.

Think of how easily your emotions can be changed by the simple things in life.

Perhaps a certain piece of music can lift your spirits ... or a walk, a piece of artwork, sex, a poem, surfing, driving, cooking, swimming, dancing, shopping, singing ... there are an infinite number of possibilities here.

Start to notice what changes your mood for the better.

Make a list of the things that energise and excite you. Now do these things!

Take Some 'Me' Time

'Me' time is spent on yourself alone. This time is not for others, it's just for you. What, you can't find the time? Well if you can't find time for yourself how can you expect anyone else to find time for you? Value yourself and your time alone and you will find that others will value you.

- Prioritise yourself

- Take a few minutes every day this week just to stand and stare

- Enjoy the chance to be yourself

- Create a regular daily slot in your diary for you to relax and just be.

You deserve this space, so take it!

— 2 —

Lighten Up

What is the difference between self-awareness and self-absorption?

When do our inner reflections and musings (why do I feel like this / act like that / think this way ...) turn into an ego-fuelled journey to a boring and selfish place?

Keep it light by remembering the following:

- You are a work in progress; you are recreating yourself, your environment and your relationships at every moment of the day.

- You can enjoy your creativity and trust your process.

- When the going gets tough you can lighten up.

- Self-awareness opens the door to change.

- You are an amazing person.

- Nothing is impossible.

Making Good Relationships

The basis of all your relationships is found in your own relationship with yourself.

- If you believe in yourself, others will reflect that belief.

- If you have high self-esteem, you will be respected.

- If you are fascinated by life, others will find you fascinating.

- If you are a loving person, others will love you.

When you are happy with yourself, your relationships will be happy.

Show Your Thanks

As we struggle to make some of our more difficult relationships work it is easy to stop putting the effort into the relationships that support us positively.

Think of that person who is always there to listen to you, and that friend who helps you to pick up the pieces.

Do you really appreciate those people who give you emotional support?

It is much too easy to take good people for granted.

Remember to show your appreciation of those people who support you – these are the most important people in your life. Find the time to show your thankfulness.

A Special List for Parents

As you enter the uncharted territory of parenthood (where many have gone before but no one has any maps!) it's good to know a few important things.

Copy this list and stick it somewhere highly visible. Look at it throughout the day:

- There are no perfect parents.
- Parenthood is a big job.
- I don't have to feel guilty.
- I need to look after myself.
- I can let go.
- I forgive and thank my mother and father.
- I am doing a good job.
- I am a good mother / father.

Parents everywhere are doing a magnificent job, we couldn't survive without you!

Celebrate Your Successes

Sometimes it seems that whatever we do is never quite good enough.

You know how it feels: you pass that exam, finish a project, reach your target weight, get that promotion you were going for ... But after all that hard work it can feel like a bit of an anticlimax, and so straight away you start to look around for your next challenge.

We expect so much more of ourselves than we do of others, and this is bound to lead to dissatisfaction.

Allow yourself to be successful by recognising and celebrating all the successes in your life.

Feel the Fear

- List three things you would love to do but have been afraid to try.

- Write down the worst possible outcomes and the best possible outcomes of doing each of these three things.

- Now ask yourself, 'What are my anxieties and fears?' Write them down.

- Ask yourself how realistic these fears are and how they compare with the best possible outcomes.

Well, how realistic are your fears? When you get right down to looking at them you will probably find that they are irrational. Feel the fear and do it anyway! You will feel amazing.

Habit Busting

Revitalise yourself by stopping your energy-zapping habits and reclaiming your balance and creativity.

- Take time each day to stop all activity and savour the silence.

- Stop saying 'yes' to everything.

- Think things through before you agree to do something. Say 'no' if you want to.

- Let yourself be human, ask for help and express your needs. You are not Superwoman or Superman, and people do like to do things for each other.

- Get your life in balance. All work and no play wrecks us physically and emotionally. Fun and relaxation are powerful energy boosters.

— 9 —

Uplifting Others

This is a great technique to use at work – notice the changes in the attitudes of your colleagues.

- Become aware of the words that you are using, in thought as well as in speech.

- Use positive energy-raising words, such as: harmony, peace, radiance, joy, inspired, delightful, wonderful ...

- Think of such positive words and concepts and all your thoughts will be uplifted.

- Speak to others using enthusiastic and inspiring words and they will feel brighter and happier.

What Do You Love?

When we truly love we can overcome our doubts and become empowered and decisive. When we feel like this our positive energy creates strong vibrations that attract new and vibrant relationships into our lives.

So what do you love that can make you feel so positive and creative? Make a list of twenty things that you absolutely love. Be specific and detailed – for example, Great Aunt Daisy's plum pudding (hot with ice-cream), the hairs on the back of your baby daughter's neck, the third track of a certain CD, falling snow in the lamplight ...

Love feelings will attract more love feelings. Write another list!

Move Your Body

There is a direct relationship between exercise and a positive mood.

So why is it that at the first mention of exercise we imagine that we have to run marathons, swim fifty lengths, lift huge weights? No wonder it all feels like too much effort.

Keeping fit does not mean that you have to become a top athlete. Nor does it mean that you need a perfect Lycra-clad body before you can get on an exercise bike. You don't even have to go near a gym when a good brisk daily walk will work wonders.

Get that body moving!

When a Relationship Ends

When a long-term relationship ends we are emotionally bruised and battered, and the prospect of a quick fling is enticing. But this isn't the best way to rebuild our shattered ego and sexual confidence.

Five ways to survive when a long-term relationship ends:

- Take care of yourself, you are worth it.
- Look for a new interest (make good use of the extra time on your hands).
- Develop platonic relationships with men / women; you may be amazed at how fulfilling non-sexual relationships can be.
- Spend more time with your friends.
- Learn to enjoy your own company.

Dance Your Worries Away

Take a few moments to try this lovely technique that will help you to get your worries in perspective.

- Sit quietly and relax your body.

- Close your eyes and let you thoughts drift away.

- Now bring to mind all your worries; see them crowding together and jostling for your attention.

- Imagine yourself clearing a pathway through the crowd. Push the worries to the side and create a shining path that leads to your future.

- Visualise yourself dancing along your path, recognising your problems as you twirl past, but not letting them stand in your way (imagine Dorothy on the Yellow Brick Road).

Tips for Training Up Your Man

- If he's throwing underpants on the floor and drinking milk straight out of the carton these are signs that he still thinks he is living with his mum. Clarify the situation for him.

- Appreciate, appreciate, appreciate (him). You will never get him to change his ways by complaining (you know this already of course). Use a subtle approach and then show your appreciation (this works like a dream).

- Continue to appreciate him in public – this builds a wonderful rapport.

- Don't give up. Domestic harmony leads to emotional harmony: a man with a mature attitude to household chores can also develop emotional maturity.

Understand Self-esteem

All human beings struggle with issues of self-esteem –
yes even those oh-so-confident-looking folk!

It seems as if our self-esteem is always on the line. We
can go up and down again with alarming speed. (Does
this sound like you?)

Our self-esteem is rather like a beautiful but very delicate
flower that needs constant nourishment and care in
order for it to grow and remain protected.

Use the tips in this book and as you cultivate ways to
bring positive changes into your life your self-esteem
will become more stable.

Like Water Off a Duck's Back

It's so easy to get knocked off our perch, isn't it? There we are feeling great and then someone criticises us and down we go into that whirlpool of negativity and lack of confidence. Who needs this?

If you feel undermined by anyone always remember this: their criticism would mean nothing to you if part of you didn't believe it to be true. If someone told you that you were a monkey you would just laugh at them, wouldn't you?

The next time someone tries to brings you down, just let it go right over you. Don't buy into their version of the truth; know your own worth!

Here Comes the Sun

It's amazing what a bit of sunshine can do to lift our spirits, but why wait for good weather in order to look on the bright side of life?

It's fascinating how one person can help raise our energy with optimism while another can ruin our day with their negativity and pessimism.

When you wake up tomorrow let your thoughts dwell on the power of your own energy. Take optimism, positivity and hope into your daily life and lift the energy around you. Keep light and bright.

You do make a difference.

Keep Your Partnership Dynamic

It has been said that a woman gets together with a man thinking that she can and will change him, whereas the man thinks that the woman will stay the same forever. No wonder the divorce rates are so high!

Here are some tips from partners who have managed to stay together through thick and thin:

- Keep dating (each other)!

- Praise much more and criticise much less – this brings fabulous results.

- Be the first to apologise.

- Never, ever, humiliate your partner in public (or in private).

- Change your routines occasionally – habits create boredom.

— 19 —

Be an Inspiration

Can you think of someone who could do with some encouragement right now? Is that person you? One of the best ways to give yourself hope is to be an inspiration for another person.

- Think of someone who gave you encouragement.

- What did they say to you?

- What did they do?

Now, do the same for someone else. Help someone to bring out their very best and you will find something quite amazing: when you inspire another person you feel inspired yourself.

We are all here to help each other; let this belief lie at the heart of all your relationships.

20

With All Your Love

This is the most fabulous technique. It's easy, direct and so powerful.

When we are feeling upbeat we can often feel even more helpless in the face of the sadness of other people. It's possible even to feel guilty about our happiness. There is no need to feel guilty, you can always act to alleviate the pain of others!

Whenever you become aware of suffering, send your love to the person / problem / disaster. Visualise your love as a beam of white light (or just know that you have sent it). There is no right or wrong way to do this. Do it your way.

Let Yourself Be Happy

It is estimated that 70 per cent of us are clinically depressed at some time in our lives. With so many opportunities available, why are we so unhappy?

People try everything: sex, career, money, marriage, divorce, alcohol, cigarettes, rock and roll, and even drugs, but most of us want only one thing – to be happy.

Happiness is a natural part of the human condition; we only need to believe this and then allow ourselves to feel it.

You deserve to be happy.

Prioritise happiness and make it your number one goal.

Remember to appreciate the joys of life.

Be grateful for the simple pleasures.

Be Happy to Do It

When we speak negatively we attract more negativity and feel even worse. Happily, the opposite is true.

Sometimes we use seemingly harmless words that can in fact have a very harmful effect on the way we feel.

- Notice that when you say you have 'got' to do something, you put yourself under unnecessary pressure.

- Watch your words carefully. Become aware whenever you say that you have 'got' to do something.

- Where possible replace 'I've got to' with 'I'm happy to'.

- Be persistent with this, it is such a brilliant tip.

Keep Learning

Let conscious learning become a way of life and it will help you to reach your very highest potential.

Every time we reach a personal learning plateau (where work and creativity are feeling stuck) we need to cross it and move on to a new level.

We cross this plateau by:

- Finding new interests that will extend and develop our skills and strengths
- Looking for support and advice when we need it
- Keeping alert and mentally active

We are never too old to learn. To keep our minds at their creative best, we must keep inputting new ideas.

Value Yourself

When we are low, we are full of self-dislike and self-criticism; there are just so many things we don't like about ourselves. Decide to love yourself today.

- Appreciate your body and all it does for you.

- Encourage yourself to try something new.

- Look at yourself in a mirror and say, 'I love and value myself.' This is hard, but stick at it for great results.

- Forgive yourself for everything you think you have done wrong. You can let yourself off the hook.

- Let every thought and action support you.

Love yourself and you will love your life!

Stop Comparison Shopping

- Do you ever use words like average or normal to describe yourself?

- Do you often wish that you looked like someone else?

- Do you try to fit in?

- Are you constantly unhappy with the size and shape of your body?

- Do you ever feel jealous of others?

- Are you afraid to rock the boat?

If we pursue the lifestyle dream of 'having it all' we will spend our whole lives trying to 'fit in' with media hype and we will always be low in self-confidence.

Be yourself! Rock the boat! Reclaim your self-esteem!

Fit for Life

A good keep-fit regime requires a commitment of time, energy and motivation, and it's easy to believe that we haven't any of these to spare.

Do you recognise any of the following excuses?:

- I find exercise so boring.
- I'm basically a lazy person.
- I haven't got the time.
- My head hurts.
- I'm too uncoordinated.
- I've been exercising for three weeks and nothing is happening.
- I'm too fat to wear Lycra.
- I can't afford to join a gym.

Don't Worry about Stress

Stress is only a word used to describe the feelings we have when we are not coping very well with our lives.

This definition helps us to get a grip on the concept of stress. How often have you felt uptight and out of control and told yourself that you are 'just feeling stressed'? But this only ever serves to add to your anxiety, doesn't it?

Forget about worrying about your stress levels and just do what needs to be done to resolve your situation.

You have all the ability you need to cope with whatever life throws at you!

When Good Women
Like Bad Men

Have you ever had a relationship with a man behaving badly? Why do we love to take emotional risks with men who don't deserve us? Why do so many women stand by their man while putting up with his verbal, psychological or even physical abuse?

Know this important fact: A woman can never change a man! So:

- Stop waiting for him to change.
- Never put up with abuse.
- Next time choose a man who is emotionally mature.

If you are fed up with being victimised in your love relationships just remember this: we attract the relationships that we think we deserve.

A Confident New You

Uptight, tense, stressed out or pressurised? Consider this: could any of these emotional states be due to a lack of confidence in you?

When life gets on top of us it means that our needs are not being met. When this happens we need to ask ourselves some serious questions, such as:

- Am I being valued at work?

- Am I looking after myself?

- Does my partner show his / her appreciation of me?

- Am I in the right job?

- Why am I discontented?

- Do I deserve to be treated well?

Be strong, be confident, and take control of your life.

Empty that Wardrobe

Have you any clothes in your wardrobe that you haven't worn for a couple of years? If so, why are you hanging on to them?

Are you keeping things because of past memories? If so, you may be unable to move forward in your life because you are stuck in the past. If this is the case get rid of them.

Perhaps you are waiting to 'grow back' into some clothes. Each time you see these 'slimmer you' clothes, you are affecting your body image. Take them to the local charity shop.

Clear out your wardrobe and your mind of old memories that are holding you back.

You Deserve It

If you don't believe that you deserve the best then you will not allow good things into your life. This negative belief may be blocking your progress.

What do you think you deserve?......................................

....

- Do you deserve to fulfil your dreams?

- Do you deserve the best that life can offer?

- Do you believe that you don't deserve very much or, in fact, that you deserve nothing at all?

Think about all the 'deserving' messages you may have internalised.

Repeat the following affirmation: I deserve the best in life.

Believe that you deserve the best and you will get it.

We Are All in This Together

As soon as we decide that we want to change, develop and grow we start a process of self-reflection which sometimes gets to feel very serious. We often have to dig deep to recognise the patterns and habits that aren't working for us and need changing; our personal challenges are a challenge!

It can sometimes feel as if we are the only one struggling away with the emotional intensity of personal issues, but of course this isn't true.

We are all in this together.

Attract that Special Person

Want to make that special person notice you? Try the
following:

- Create conversational intimacy. Introduce 'we'
  statements early on in the relationship (we
  could go there / we both seem to enjoy ...) and
  the other person will begin to feel that you are
  already close.

- Hold their gaze when you are making eye
  contact. Unbroken eye contact stimulates the
  release of phenylethylamine, which can
  heighten a sense of infatuation.

- Empathise. Use phrases such as 'I understand',
  'Well done', 'You are right'.

If he / she is slow to reciprocate, think again: are they
worth the effort?

In Praise of a Child

Each time we recognise children in a positive way we are empowering them. Positive support helps them to develop confidence and self-esteem.

Using praise is a powerful way to help a child feel good about herself or himself. So if you haven't got a child of your own, go out and find one (nephew, niece, godchild, next-door neighbour, stranger in another street ...). There are plenty about and they are all very receptive to praise!

This is such a great thing to do because you get a really special feeling when you encourage a child to feel good inside – everyone gets a warm glow, you too!

Just Scream!

When your stress levels are high, your confidence drops.

You can let go of stress by screaming your head off.

- Go and find a private quiet spot.

- Now stretch your mouth as wide as you can and tense the muscles in your face, neck and head. (The rest of your body may feel pretty tense too.)

- Then, clench your fists and beat the air and scream ... silently!

- Relax totally, feel all your muscles droop and go limp, and then repeat the routine.

Watch Your Words

- Write down all the things you think you should do, for example: I should get a better job.

- Now, look at each 'I should' on your list and read it out loud.

- Then ask yourself, 'Why should I?'

- Rewrite your list, replacing 'should' with 'could' and start each statement with, 'If I really wanted to', for example: If I really wanted to I could get a better job.

Eradicate 'should' from your speech and thoughts; it always implies guilt in some way. Replace 'should' with 'could' and give yourself the opportunity to change. Don't ever be victimised by the words you use.

— 7 —

Do It Now

Research has shown that people who always put off until tomorrow what they could do today are more likely to suffer from stress than those who stick to deadlines.

So stop procrastinating.

- Think of a task or a difficulty that you keep putting off tackling.
- How much time and energy do you spend worrying about it?
- Do you feel guilty?
- How do you feel about yourself for not getting it done?
- Is procrastination worth all this pain?
- List all that you need to do.
- Seize the moment – NOW!

Soul Connections

Our creative energy is at its peak when our mind, body and spirit are working in harmony. Connect with your spiritual energy and feel a new creative surge.

- Sit down, relax and close your eyes.

- Place your right hand over your heart and say to yourself, 'I breathe the soul's breath.'

- Exhale until your lungs feel empty.

- Now wait until your breath naturally comes to you to fill the space.

- When you feel your breath come to you in this way you are breathing the soul's breath.

- Keep practising and open up to your spiritual energy.

Letting Go of Cellulite

We are our own worst enemies when it comes to body confidence and self-image. If we are sincere in our declaration that we are only trying to look good for our own sakes then surely we can let go of our obsession with cellulite?

Let's remove our dimply bits from under the microscope of our attention and focus on something more meaningful. Rather than asking, 'Why have I got cellulite?' you could ask, 'What is the real meaning of my life?'

Get your life in perspective and focus on realising your amazing potential. There is so much more to life than smooth undimpled skin!

More Tips for Success at Work

1 Keep believing in yourself and others will value and appreciate you.

2 See your so called 'problems' as 'opportunities' for you to rise to a new challenge.

3 Be committed and focused. The difference between the winners and the losers is only ever about attitude and approach.

4 You can change your mind. Life has a way of throwing the unexpected in our paths, so be ready to make contingency plans and let go of preconceived ideas that are no longer appropriate.

5 Use good open communication skills at all times; good work comes from people who feel valued.

Five-minute Meditation

- Sit comfortably with your eyes closed and watch your mind at work: just let it wander.

- Notice how full of thoughts you are.

- Ignore them. They will keep coming, just take no notice of them.

- Concentrate on the rhythm of your breathing.

- Become aware of your breathing. As you breathe in, think 'in', and as you breathe out, think 'out'.

- Every time your mind drifts off just come back to your breathing.

- Become aware of the place between the breaths.

- Keep returning to this point.

- When you are ready, come back gently into to your body.

Coping with Nerves

Cast your mind back to the last time you were faced with a group of strangers – perhaps at a party, a work-training event or a job interview.

Faced with the unknown our adrenaline starts rushing and our behaviour can become erratic.

The person who can survive the pressure is the one who has high self-esteem and feels free to be herself or himself.

Everyone feels intimidated sometimes in their lives. The person who survives such feelings is the one who has an open mind and can see the lighter side of life.

Keep it light and spontaneous and your butterflies will fly away.

Sadness and Loss

Ways to cope with sadness and loss:

- Know that your feelings are natural, acknowledge them and express them – this is the way forward.

- People are brave, amazing and strong and they bounce back from adversity. Never forget this.

- Take heart from the courage of others.

- Appreciate your loved ones, know how much they mean to you and tell them!

- Find something that gives you hope and know that you will feel optimistic again.

- Look for what brings real meaning to your life.

- Believe that you will laugh and enjoy life again, because you will!

A Think Slim Day

You know those days when you wake up feeling lethargic, bloated, overfed and way down in the attraction stakes?

Get a grip on your day and turn it into a 24-hour programme to take off a little weight, make you feel spiritually lighter and more in control, and boost your feelings of self-respect.

- Keep your diet as light and pure as you can.

- Drink tepid water with lemon juice every couple of hours to detoxify your system.

- Plan some exercise time and relaxation time throughout the day.

Tomorrow you will wake up feeling better, brighter and lighter!

We are Here to Learn

So learn! You are that baby with the adventurous spirit who taught herself / himself to walk. Remember this when the going gets hard and the emotional risks seem overwhelming.

Do something adventurous today. Do the one thing that you have been longing to do but too afraid to try. Visualise yourself scrambling up from the floor once more, determined to walk. Reclaim your determination and focus and embrace your so-called failures and mistakes. Learn a new trick and move on out into a new reality.

Spread Your Light Around

We are all energetically connected to each other and affect each other.

Your energetic contribution counts! Try this:

- The next time you recognise that someone else is struggling, send them light.

- Visualise them surrounded by light (enlightening them and lightening their load).

- If you are having problems with anyone then mentally shower them with light.

If you find visualisation difficult, just the thought of sending light is enough. Let go of all doubts about how it works; believe me, it works!

Spread your light around today and notice how you start to feel.

Your Perfect Body

Ask anybody you know (the thin, the fat, the gorgeous, the plain) if they are happy with their body and they will give you a great list of complaints. Women (and increasingly men) are feeling pressurised to become something they cannot be.

We must fight back and subdue this inclination to dislike our bodies.

- When you next see a glamorous, glossy image of a body, don't start to compare yourself.

- Don't go down that self-critical path.

- Your own body is a perfect machine, but it won't run happily if you start hating it.

Your Best Shot

You are feeling challenged beyond your usual limits. What to do? How to act? What to do with the stress?

- Face the challenge.
- Assess the situation.
- Decide what you can do (realistically).
- Act on your decision.
- Give it your best shot.
- Let go of 'what ifs'.
- Trust your action.
- Trust that the universe will support you.
- Let go and move on.

Your best shot is just that! So now it's time to let go and move on, knowing that you did everything you could.

Congratulate Yourself

Congratulate yourself for recognising that you have the personal power to change the quality of your life. As you tap into all these positive tips your life will begin to transform.

Your empowerment is your birthright, but you have to work for it and the work is not always easy. Sometimes it feels impossible to believe in yourself, but never doubt your progress, even when darkness seems to engulf you. Know that all the love and support you need will always be with you.

The darkest hour really is just before the dawn, and you will come shining through!

De-stress

Whenever you are stressed or your nerves are just jangling, it's time to get grounded.

- Sit or stand with your feet apart, soles flat on the ground.
- Close your eyes.
- Become aware of the energy points at the centre of the soles of both your feet.
- Feel the gentle tugging of the earth on your feet.
- Visualise the connection. Imagine roots leading from these energy points, way down into the centre of the earth. You are connected!
- Feel the pull of the earth.
- Feel that your energy is grounded, centred and focused.

Find Your Inner Child

When life feels dull and boring you need to seek a new pair of eyes. Forget your jaded cynicism and bring some wonder back into your life.

Re-create some favourite childhood experiences: make a sandcastle, paddle in the sea, eat a sherbet dip, go on a carousel ride, smell the candyfloss (and eat it) ... as you bite into that toffee apple you are the child within you.

Do at least one playful thing every day and watch the experience grow on you. This world is a wonderful place and your life is a miracle.

The Very Best Medicine

Smiling and laughter really do have amazing health benefits, as well as lifting our mood and making us feel great.

Laughing is wonderful exercise: it deepens our breathing and improves our circulation, and smiles and laughter stimulate the production of our natural feel-good chemicals. So why not take your good mood out and about and share it with others who need a boost?

Put a smile on your face, go for laughter and put even more positive energy out into the world. You will feel fabulous and so will everyone around you.

Being Perfect

I know if I can do it just one more time, I can get it completely right. When it's totally perfect I will be content; when I lose more weight, then I will be happy; I must look absolutely right; the house must be immaculate; I need to cook a first-class meal; everything must be totally together ... I must be Superwoman (or Superman)!

- Do you recognise yourself here?
- Do you set yourself standards by which you judge the value of your days?
- Are you always striving to achieve more?

Give yourself a break. Perfectionists are never winners.

Assertiveness Quiz

- Do you ever feel taken for granted?

- Do you feel appreciated by your partner and / or family?

- Do you always work late if asked, even if it's inconvenient?

- When salespeople ring you at home do you always listen to what they have to say even if you're not interested?

- Do you ever find yourself apologising for your behaviour?

- Do you ever just pay a bill even if you think you have been overcharged?

- Are you afraid of what people think about you?

Is it time you stood up for yourself?

Women Are from Venus

... and men speak another language.

Never forget that men and women are different and that men are unable to use both sides of their brain at the same time! This physiological fact has an important effect on women's relationships with men because it means that men can be logical or emotional but they can't make spontaneous connections with their feelings and their rationality, so they cannot express their emotions as they are feeling them.

Use your knowledge of our gender differences to smooth and harmonise your relationships with men and enjoy our diversity.

Vive la différence!

An Action Plan
for Self-esteem

Use these six tips and feel the difference in your life.

1 Never ever bring yourself down; always look
   for your positive points.

2 Practise saying 'no' to yourself in the mirror –
   then go out and do it for real!

3 Think of something you have been putting off
   doing – then do it (you will feel great about
   yourself).

4 Be your own best friend; be kind and
   thoughtful to yourself – you are worth it.

5 Take a few moments just for yourself every
   day – you deserve it!

6 Keep believing in yourself.

Creating Amazing Realities

We create our own reality, and the quality of the life we create depends on our self-image.

How do you see yourself?

How does this affect your life?

Self-critical thoughts create low self-esteem.

Create new and improved realities by making your self-image positively affirming. Read each of the following affirmations and simultaneously visualise them coming true for you.

- I am strong and powerful.

- I am intelligent and resourceful.

- My body is beautiful.

- Everything I do is a success.

Let Go of Guilt

Guilt destroys good feelings; it's like a strong acid that burns away at self-respect. We often have a close relationship with irrational guilt, and this keeps us in a no-win situation. Guilt will destroy your self-esteem unless you decide to erase it from your life.

Try the following:

> Make the affirmation *I am always doing my best* while visualising any guilty feelings floating away in a bubble, never to be seen again.

Keep practising letting go of guilt and it will get easier and easier to do as your life gets easier and easier to live.

Everything Changes

By the time you get to this end of this sentence, 100,000 of your cells will have died. You will be on the way to becoming someone else!

Yes, everything is changing all of the time, including you. Although we know this is true, we can spend a lot of energy trying to hang on to the illusion that everything stays the same. Recognise the transitory nature of life and adopt the following habits:

- Go with the flow.
- Stay flexible.
- Keep an open mind.
- Allow yourself to change.

Going Through It

When do motivational words fire you with enthusiasm and fill you with a new sense of direction and when do they just tip you into further negativity? Positivity can sometimes be so hard to take, can't it?

If you're feeling fragile and a bit low today, don't try to force yourself to be full of beans. Take it easy. Don't beat yourself up; just let yourself off the hook.

Sometimes we have to see a mood through (it's called going through it). And when it's over we can pick up on the positive tips once again.

Recognise Your Believing Mirrors

Do you spend a lot of time and energy trying to make poor relationships work? Why not use that time to work on your relationships with people who support you?

Who tells you: 'Yes you can do that', 'Go on, have a go at it, you have nothing to lose', 'I'm here if you need me to help you'? Make a list of all the people in your life who support you and encourage you. These people reflect your true potential and will themselves be positive thinkers who are well-focused and able to mirror back to you all of your own possibilities.

Recognise your believing mirrors: they reflect your highest dreams.

It's Safe to Trust

When we can trust ourselves (our own decisions, behaviour, thoughts) we also find it easy to trust other people. And the more we can show others that we trust and are committed to them, the more positively they will respond.

- Share your trusting feelings with others in your life, in particular those who are struggling right now.

- Give them the benefit of the doubt.

- Let them fulfil your positive expectations of them.

- Bring the feeling of trust into the lives of others and your own good feelings will develop even more.

You Are Unique

Do you ever compare yourself with others? Do you ever feel that you are 'not as good as' someone else or not sufficiently worthy / thin / clever / happy / talented?

- Whenever you compare yourself with someone else you are behaving like a victim, with low self-esteem.

- Never forget that you are unique.

- There will never be another person on the planet who is just like you.

- You are original and you are special.

- Let your uniqueness shine through.

Just the Way You Are

If only I could lose weight, get a better job, pass that exam, become a better parent, be more intelligent, go to the gym more ... then I could like myself.

I only need to be better, feel better, look better and then I will be a worthwhile person.

If you recognise this train of thought as one of yours, then STOP!

If you are looking for perfection you will never find it: you will never be 'good enough' to accept yourself. You are FABULOUS, AMAZING, ORIGINAL and FANTASTIC just the way you are.

The Art of Living

As we work on ways to increase our self-belief and self-esteem we begin to recognise that there is an art to feeling good about ourselves and our world. You will discover many of these art-forms for yourself along the way, but for now here are a few hot tips for you:

- Forgive.
- Appreciate.
- Let go of blame.
- Take personal responsibility.
- Know that the universe supports you.
- Love your life and it will love you back.
- Spread happiness.
- Be yourself.

Take One Step at a Time

Every day doesn't start with a bang; sometimes it's hard just to find the energy to get out of bed.

Whatever the reason for your slow start there is only one way to cope, and that is to take your day one step at a time.

- Concentrate on the immediate task in hand.
- Just get yourself out of bed, don't think of the next job.
- Stay in the moment, just doing what needs to be done.
- Before you know it you will be up and running.

As you achieve more tasks you will start to regain control.

Think Prosperously

Create abundance and prosperity in your life.

When our energy is depressed it is so easy to lock into a view of the world based on scarcity. It can seem that life is a competitive struggle for scarce resources. This worldview has created the problems that we face today.

- Think abundantly.
- Think inclusively.
- Think co-operatively.
- Think of each other.

We are all connected and our world is naturally prolific. There is plenty of everything to go round if we don't interfere with nature's plans. We have created the concept of scarcity; let's create abundance and prosperity instead.

Are You a Winner?

- Do you feel that your life is a success story or have you lost out in some way?

- Do you achieve your goals or do you feel like a victim?

- Are you reaching your full potential or are you dissatisfied with your lot?

What exactly does it mean to be a winner?

Winning is not always about being first, but it is about always giving your best in every situation. When you strive to reach your potential you will feel successful and confident; you will feel like a winner!

Your Deepest Truth

When you are being true to yourself you stand by your own values and live their reality. If you find yourself being manipulated by others you are able to be true to your own feelings and be assertive.

Feeling victimised is a sign that you have not stood by your own beliefs and your deepest truth.

Your deep spiritual connection reminds you that you are first and foremost a spiritual being who is learning to be human.

Never forget that you are rooted in spirit and in love and that you have your own perfect place in this world.

Creating Happiness

No, you can't buy satisfaction but you can create it. You have the power to change your own life for the better. Decide to start now!

- Take a pen and a piece of paper and write along the top 'Six Things I Most Want to Do in My Life'.

- Write your list.

- Now, look at each of your items and ask yourself this question: 'Am I working towards doing any of these things?'

- Recognise your dreams and then begin to make them happen.

You can never buy a happy life, you can only achieve it.

PMA at Work

You are only as stressed as you believe you are.

It's all the rage to be stressed, but stress always lies in the eye of the beholder. When life at work starts getting to you, don't let yourself become a 'stress victim' who blames their job for all their negative mental states.

Use a **P**ositive **M**ental **A**pproach to deal with difficult work scenarios and keep your mood bright and friendly. And keep in mind that if you are still feeling pressurised after all this effort, it may be worth considering a career change!

Just for Women

Women are different from men! Women in groups can offer each other such a wealth of emotional support, laughter, stress release and physical support.

There are some aspects of our being that we can't or don't want to share with men, and this is quite right and natural.

So go out and find a class in aerobics, line-dancing, yoga, pottery, massage, aromatherapy ... or join a book-reading group (or whatever appeals to you) for the benefit of the mutual support you will find. There are lots of women attending all sorts of classes – go and find a group for yourself.

Women can empower themselves in relationships with other women.

Body Talk

Our body language reflects what we are feeling; what is yours saying about you?

When our confidence is low our shoulders droop, we avoid eye contact and all our bits and pieces start to sag! If we change our body messages so that they are more assertive we will automatically feel more confident.

Next time you are feeling low, sit up straight with your shoulders back and maintain eye contact with others. This physical shift alone can start to move you out of your negativity.

Look more assertive and you will feel it, and others will respond to your increased feelings of self-respect.

Letting Go Sets You Free

Why do we feel that we cannot really fully enjoy anything unless we can own it? Think about how this attitude can affect our relationships with people as well as with the objects that we can buy.

The more we can let go of our attachments, the clearer and happier our lives become. We may think that if we let go of things and people then we will have nothing, but, amazingly, the opposite is true. Letting go sets us free, and everything that is truly yours will always come back to you.

Take that Brave New Step

Do you want something new in your life? Are you looking for change? Then act!

Don't even stop to face your fears, just jump right over them, leave them way behind and don't look back. Action speaks louder than words, so make that first move and then just keep at it.

When you take a brave new step forward you are never alone. The universe always supports and endorses courage and decisive behaviour: radiate boldness and you will attract all the positive and powerful energy that you need.

Get your head out of the sand and act!

Get that Loving Feeling

When was the last time you fell in love? Didn't it feel amazing? What bliss to be able to feel like that all the time!

Believe me, you can feel like this without falling in love with someone new every day. You only need to nurture your relationship with yourself.

- Put yourself first.
- Take time and space to be alone.
- Give yourself gifts and treats.
- Appreciate yourself totally – mind, body and soul.
- Learn to love your own company.

Before we are able to love others, we must learn to love ourselves.

Stop Competing

Each and every human achievement demonstrates the incredible potential open to us all. But if we run a competitive race with others we will constantly lose, because someone will always come along who can improve on our performance.

- Learn from the achievements of other people and add this knowledge to your own experience.

- Know that the human potential is amazing. We are so much more incredible than we think we are.

- Enjoy the fantastic possibilities instead of being defeated by them.

- Everyone's success adds to your success. Remember that we are all in this together.

Ignore Your Inner Critic

Most of us find it so much easier to be self-critical than to praise ourselves. That part of us which nags away and is never, ever satisfied by our performance (it could have been so much better!) is called the 'Inner Critic'.

If you are always bringing yourself down, stop the next time you catch yourself doing this. Now look closely at your beliefs. Are you really useless / lazy / stupid / never good enough ...?

Ninety-nine per cent of the time you will have been listening to your Inner Critic. Ignore its nagging voice. Have no doubt: you are amazing!

A Passionate Life

Showing your feelings is a fabulous way to get what you want in life. When we are passionate about things, we are enthusiastic, dynamic and completely lacking in self-consciousness and timidity.

Passion takes us outside of ourselves and allows our energy to flow in a purposeful and attractive way. Then we are at our most creative.

- Don't be reluctant to show your feelings.
- Trust your instincts and follow your star.
- Be enthusiastic and watch the world respond.
- Overcome shyness with excitement.

What do you really love to do?

Love of life creates a loving life.

Creating Your Reality

When you are feeling empowered always recognise the part you have played in creating this feeling of well-being. And when you find your self-esteem falling, always recognise the part you have played in this also.

It is sometimes easier to blame circumstances, others, the weather, politicians or whatever for our downbeat mood.

But you alone are responsible for your awareness.

You can always change your mood by changing your attitude.

If a way of looking at the world is not working for you, then look at it a different way!

Value Your Team

Are you aware of your team members? Do you even know who is part of your team?

I'm not talking about your local football team but about any group of people who work and co-operate with you.

You probably belong to any number of teams: your family, drama group, work team, sports club, parent group at school ... Make a list of them all.

Being part of a team encourages our sense of wellbeing and belonging. There is nothing quite like that feeling of shared achievement.

Think about your teams and value your team members. Show them how much you appreciate them.

This Is It!

This isn't a dummy run or a dress rehearsal. You will never repeat this precious moment. This is the real thing! Use your positive mood to make sure that you are running on all cylinders.

Ask yourself these questions:

- Am I living my life to the full?
- Do I make the most of every moment?
- Do I appreciate the wonder and beauty that surrounds me?
- If I had four weeks left to live what would I have to say to whom?
- Say it now.

Love your life completely. Live like there was no tomorrow, because there may not be.

Tips for Looking Good

- Remember that lack of sexual confidence is a common syndrome – you are not alone.

- Being comfortable with yourself is the key to body confidence.

- Love and appreciate your body, whatever its shape and size. You are unique and special.

- Sexual confidence is the finest aphrodisiac of all: know yourself, know what you want and don't be afraid to ask for it.

- Make the very best of yourself – you are worth it!

- Never ever forget that those glossy images of perfection are not real: don't compare yourself with airbrushed pictures of glamorous beauties.

Through the Eyes of Love

There are two ways of looking at the world, through the eyes of love or the eyes of fear.

When you are positive, upbeat, hopeful, appreciative, forgiving and open-hearted you are coming from your deepest truth; you are coming from love. This is a place where you are able to express your feelings and feel self-respect and self-worth.

- Live your truth.
- Stand by your ideals,
- Treat others with respect.

Love and appreciate yourself and others, and the realities you create will be wondrous and joyful.

Your Dreams Come True

Money brings financial security, and that is all it brings. It doesn't make us more confident or improve our relationships and it doesn't make our dreams come true. Our deep-down dreams are not about luxury yachts and diamonds, rather they are about personal potential and fulfilment.

- Are you getting what you want from life?

- Do you enjoy your job?

- Are your relationships harmonious?

- How is your social life?

- Are you high in self-esteem?

- Is there a spring in your step?

There is only one way to make your dreams come true and that is to start living them ... now.

How to Win Life's Prizes

- Treat others with respect and consideration and this will be returned to you.

- Always find something good to say about someone and you will stay in a positive cycle.

- Become the friend that you would most like to have and you will be amazed by how your relationships improve.

- Remember that money can't buy love and happiness.

- Encourage and inspire others and your own self-esteem will rise.

- Maintain your integrity and you will always be able to trust yourself.

- Always behave in the best way you can: your behaviour is a measure of the sort of person you are.

The Smile in Your Pocket

Our normal day-to-day existence can often feel so ordinary and mundane – getting up / looking after children / going to work / shopping / vacuuming / watching TV / making dinner / putting out the rubbish ... When we are so routinised we can become bored, dissatisfied and miserable, and then we take ourselves too seriously.

When you catch yourself in this mood, remember what my dear old granddad used to say: 'Girl, there's always a smile in your pocket.' That always made me laugh.

Lighten the load, put on that smile and feel the difference.

When the Going
Gets Tough

Everywhere we look people are telling us to just be positive and not to be so negative, as if our personal problems could be waved away with a magic wand. But being positive does not mean pretending to be OK when you are not. We need to be positively aware of our difficulties so that we can face them head on, deal with them and move on.

When the going gets tough, the tough get positive. There is no protection as strong as the power of positive thought. Keep believing in yourself and know that the dark times will pass.

Now Is the Time

For anyone who is procrastinating (waiting for when the time is right to reach for their dreams), the news is: now is the right time!

We can all find plenty of reasons not to take that rather scary and risky next step into something new. But the longer we wait to act, the more paralysed we become, until the dream becomes a fantasy and stays one forever.

Let today be the day when you make something new happen in your life. What? You can't do it today because ...? Oh yes, you can. Step right into the centre of your life.

Just do it!

Let Go of Addictive Relationships

You are in an addictive relationship if emotions, thoughts and situations keep repeating themselves, making you feel anxious and unhappy. You may even recognise recurring physical types in your life (hair colour, hair-style, body shape, height and so on).

We can never move on, grow and fulfil our potential if we stay stuck in addictive relationships, however hard we justify them to ourselves: 'he treats me badly but I know he needs me really', 'she's still a good friend even though she is always bringing me down'.

Break away from any negative dependencies and go for positive, constructive relationships.

You Are Special

We are all different; there is no such thing as a normal type or an average-sized person. You are absolutely unique and special, so enjoy your originality.

The relationship that you have with yourself is the most important one you will ever have, so celebrate your individuality.

Once we recognise our separateness we can sometimes feel our aloneness.

- Accept and value your sense of aloneness.
- Develop an understanding relationship with yourself. When you can appreciate yourself fully, your relationships will improve dramatically.
- Value and respect yourself and others will value and respect you.

Know Yourself

Who do you think you are?

Sometimes when you feel lacking in confidence it is because you have (temporarily) lost sight of your true self. When you feel like this just check to see if you have been so busy fulfilling other people's wishes that you have forgotten your own needs.

Reclaim yourself. Find the person you really are by completing the following statements:

- I wish that I ....
- I have a deep desire to ....
- The thing I most regret is ....
- If only I could ....
- Tomorrow I am going to change the way I
  ....

Trust Your Inner Wisdom

Whenever you feel in conflict and don't know which way to turn for help, just remember that you have access to all the answers you need.

The solutions to your problems lie deep inside you.

Relax, close your eyes and try the following:

- Mentally state your problem and then ask your Inner Wisdom for guidance.

- Listen and wait. You may see or hear something that will guide you.

- Don't worry if you don't feel any change, help is at hand.

- Open your eyes and know this to be true – trust your Inner Wisdom.

Be Glad

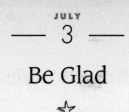

We need to remember to be glad to be alive; sometimes we just take the gift of our life for granted.

Use this technique when you are feeling down.

- Appreciate your positivity today.
- Feel gratitude for all that life gives.
- List the things that you most appreciate.
- Keep this list, pin it up on the wall and keep adding to it.
- If you run out things, go outside and take a look at the clouds, the stars, a rose, a bird ... the miracle of nature.

The more we love, the better we feel!

You Are on a Mission

Why do you think you are here? What is your mission? To ensure that your children are confident and secure? To write poetry? To bring positivity into people's lives? To live your best life?

- Remember that you have your own unique set of skills and strengths and you came here to use your abilities.

- Believe this, and then discover what drives you from within.

- Match your inner drives with action and give your life new purpose and definition.

You are here on a mission, or maybe a number of missions. Fulfil them!

Look Beyond the Image

Look in the mirror and then look beyond the image of yourself. What do you see?

- Appreciate the shape of your hands and all they do for you.
- Appreciate your beautiful smile.
- Appreciate your hair.
- Appreciate your senses.
- Appreciate your mind.
- Appreciate the life that flows through you.

You are so much more than you think you are. You are more than your appearance, more than your mind, more than your thoughts. Look beyond your image and see your spiritual energy. Spiritual energy flows through you and gives you life, never forget this!

Feeling Unattractive?

Whenever you are feeling low in the attraction stakes just take this brilliant tip from Judy Garland who said,

'Always be a first-rate version of yourself, instead of a second-rate version of somebody else.'

While you will probably make a poor imitation of Catherine Zeta Jones, you can make a sensational version of the real you. When you are at ease with yourself that confidence gives you allure and appeal beyond any new make-up formula or designer dress.

A self-assured person who is doing their own thing and not trying to impress anyone is always attractive (regardless of weight, shape or the size of their nose).

Feel At Peace

Feel calm, centred and at peace with the Basic Breath.

1 Sit on the edge of a chair. Hold your hands around your lower abdomen.

2 Deflate your stomach by exhaling fully.

3 Inhale very slowly, with your mouth closed, and feel your lower abdomen swelling in your hands.

4 Visualise the area from your groin to your ribcage as a beautiful coloured balloon, and watch it inflate slowly, filling from the bottom.

5 Expand your balloon fully and hold for three seconds.

6 Exhale slowly, watching the balloon deflate, until your abdomen is flat.

7 Repeat slowly ten times.

Your Want List

If your intimate relationship is not all that you would wish it to be (the man / woman in your life just isn't coming up with the goods), something has to crack and that doesn't have to be you.

If you are fed up with living with an ostrich (with his / her head in the sand or the newspaper) it's time to come clean with your want list.

- Write a list of your relationship wants, for example: I want more emotional support, I want you to help around the house, I want to go out with you once a week ...

- Reveal the list (being very diplomatic).

Reaping What We Sow

What goes around comes around: if we are kind and thoughtful we will attract others who behave in this way; if we are dishonest with others then how can we trust ourselves?

The quality of our life depends upon the way we live it. People may gain power, influence and money by misbehaving towards others but they will never win life's real prizes in this way. Wherever you go you cannot escape yourself, so become the person you would be happy to live with for the rest of you life.

Life will bring contentment and joy only if you sow the right seeds.

Firm Up Your Bottom

Do this before breakfast and again before dinner (and any time in between). Make a habit of doing this little exercise and you can expect a firmer bottom in a few weeks.

1 Put a chair against a wall. Stand in front of it, extending both arms in front of you and keeping your head straight.

2 As you count to five, lower yourself slowly into the chair, keeping your back straight, your arms outstretched and your chin level.

3 Count to five as you raise yourself back to the standing position.

The more frequently you do this exercise, the quicker the results.

Ten Easy Ways to Change

1 Say what you mean rather than what you think people want you to say.

2 Believe that you deserve the best, because you do!

3 Stay away from people who bring you down.

4 Forgive yourself for your mistakes (we all make mistakes).

5 Do something you have never done before.

6 Remember what you loved to do ten years ago – do it now!

7 Decide to make one of your dreams come true.

8 Spend time with positive people.

9 Learn a new skill.

10 Allow yourself to enjoy your life.

Deal With Conflict

Research has revealed that partners who are unhappy often believe that arguing is destructive. This isn't true. Conflict is a natural and inevitable part of an intimate relationship, but we need to be able to deal with it effectively.

- Choose a time when tempers have cooled and you are both feeling more relaxed.

- Negotiate (don't let problems build up).

- Just own and express your emotions (don't be critical).

- Keep your communications positive and light (if you bring each other down you will never resolve anything).

- Try to show appreciation for each other's efforts to come to some agreement.

Enjoy Your Journey

Expectations and goals are great, but watch that you are not getting into the Paradise Syndrome. This is a condition where nothing is ever enough and so we go on chasing impossible fantasies, forever feeling dissatisfied.

Take it easy, have plans but be flexible. That fantastic feeling that gives us energy and motivation comes from our ability to appreciate and really make the most of every moment. Fulfilling your self-expectations will give you confidence, but as you take each step along the way do not forget to enjoy your journey.

Satisfaction, fulfilment and happiness come from within. Love your life and it will love you back.

Leave Your Worries Behind

Do you ever feel weighed down by your problems? Of course you do. We carry around our worries and negative thoughts as if they were some important baggage that we dare not put down.

Whenever you feel tense and your mind is full of concern, stop for a moment, wherever you are.

- Visualise yourself holding large, heavy suitcases of negative emotions (no wonder you feel so drained!)
- Put them down on the ground.
- Now see yourself walking away from them.
- Leave your worries behind you; they can wreck your life.

Be a Pleasure Seeker

Are you surrounded by pleasure seekers or a lot of complainers and moaners?

Would you describe yourself as a pleasure seeker or are you waiting for pleasure to come and knock at your door? It won't, you have to go out and look for it.

- What makes your heart leap and puts a spring in your step?

- Recognise these experiences and nurture them.

- Know how to create pleasure and then you can do it whenever you wish.

- Make relationships with positive people.

- Expect pleasure and seek pleasure and you will find it.

Speak to Yourself Positively

Do you ever say things like:

- I can't do that.
- I'm useless.
- Trust me to mess up.

When you speak about yourself in a negative tone others will soon start to agree with you. Wonderful opportunities will pass you by: who wants to give that top job to someone who always messes up?

Make sure that you speak positively about yourself. Make statements like: 'I'm getting better at ...', 'I always learn from my mistakes', 'I'll do the very best I can'. Be positive, feel confident and notice the changes in the way others respond to you.

Stamp Out Stress

Releasing negative emotions through the feet is a brilliant way to let go of stress. It's used by children (adults call it having a tantrum), joggers, runners (including runners on treadmills) and those who dance to express emotions and influence events.

Feeling fed-up, frustrated, angry?

Stamp it out, grunting noisily every time your feet hit the ground!

- Bend forwards from your waist, knees slightly bent, and legs and arms dangling loosely.

- Slowly jump around, as heavily as you can, landing on both feet. Keep limp from the waist up.

- Grunt deeply 'ugh ugh' (yes really!) each time you land.

Welcome the Chores

'I must put out the rubbish, mow the lawn, clean the house, carry the shopping in … Oh no! All that lifting and bending I have to do, I'm totally exhausted just thinking about it.'

Does this sound like you?

Honestly, it's enough to tire you out before you start.

Think of it another way.

Every single exercise opportunity allows you to tone your muscles, burn calories, increase your feel-good endorphin level, and improve circulation and oxygen uptake. Some people pay a lot of money for these opportunities! Never mind the gym, you can do it all in your own home.

Set Your Goals

If you got into a car and didn't know where you were going, you would never know when you got there.

If we don't have clear goals how can we ever achieve anything? How can we measure our successes in the world?

Achieve your goals.

- Identify three short-term goals (achievable in two weeks or less).

- Make them real by getting them down on paper.

- Give yourself realistic deadlines and write these down too.

- Stick to the deadlines and reward yourself with a real prize when you reach your goal.

- You are now ready to go for a long-term goal.

Pamper Yourself

You deserve a wonderful treat. Give yourself a whole day of indulgences; enjoy a health farm extravaganza in the peace and quiet of your own home.

Plan your day

- Buy all the toiletries and beauty items you will need.
- Select some relaxing music to play.
- Choose your favourite aromatherapy oils to burn.
- Buy some delicious nutritious food, and fruit juices and/or spring water.
- Begin your day by unplugging phones and switching off all electrical distractions.

Pamper yourself all day, you deserve it. This may become a good habit!

Sex, Sex and More Sex?

- Are you a hot sexy siren with a fabulous figure and all the time and money in the world to pamper yourself?

- Are you oozing sex appeal and body confidence?

- Are you always full of zest and vitality, ready to jump into bed with your partner for a night of passionate love-making?

Sexy images are everywhere: perfect youthful bodies and faces surround us, on TV, in magazines, on the Tube, on the bus, wherever we go.

Be true to yourself and don't try to compete with these glossy images, because you will always fail.

Breathe Deeply
and ... Relax

The way we breathe actually has a direct link with the way we think, feel and act. For example, most of us breathe between 12 and 18 times a minute (and more when we are anxious and stressed). But, amazingly, if we can reduce our breaths to nine a minute or less, this will automatically increase our feelings of self-respect and self-control.

Slow and complete breathing:

- Calms and oxygenates the body.
- Removes any build-up of toxins from the body.
- Lowers the heart and pulse rate.
- Increases levels of self-esteem!

Get breathing slowly and deeply, and just relax!

What Women Want

In the film *What Women Want* Mel Gibson plays an ad man who can read the minds of the women around him. Three things spring to mind immediately:

1 Men don't have to wait until they develop telepathic powers to know what women want (they can always ask us).

2 Would we want men to know exactly what we are thinking?

3 Surely all that matters is that we know what we want. And this is the most important point.

We can only get what we want when we know what we want.

A Day of Inspiration

If we focus on misery and despair we will see it and feel it everywhere. But we can be sympathetic without becoming depressed if we focus on the strength of human courage, commitment and endurance.

So let this be a day on which you search for inspiring stories. Listen for the upbeat person wherever you are (at the checkout, bus stop, school gates, office, petrol station). Before you know it, you will be feeling inspired yourself.

Yes, anything is possible!

- Think about a change that you would like to make.
- Know that you can make positive changes.
- Commit yourself to appropriate action.

One-minute Face-lift

Use this pressure-point massage technique to stimulate the circulation to your skin, energise your facial tissues and give your face an instant lift.

1 Press lightly with your fingertips between your eyes on either side of your nose. Move up to your eyebrows, pressing as you go.

2 Press along your eyebrows.

3 Apply pressure at the outside corner of your eyes.

4 Apply pressure at your temples.

5 Move to under your eyes, pressing your way down to the centre of your cheeks.

Press downwards towards your mouth, stopping at your gum-line. Press and move to the outside edges of your jaw and press again.

Get in Touch with Your Feelings

Our society does not encourage us to express our feelings, and men usually struggle even more than women in this area.

You may be in a close relationship with someone who has denied their feelings for so long that they don't even know what they are feeling any more.

If we are out of touch with our feelings we are not being true to our own needs and so we will be low in self-esteem.

Give yourself some feeling checks throughout the day. Whenever you remember, stop for a moment and ask yourself, 'What am I feeling now?'

Practise this technique and you will boost your self-awareness.

Say What You Need

Are you disappointed by the people in your life? Do they do what you want them to do? Do they give you attention and tender loving care when you need it most, or are they always letting you down?

Does life disappoint you? Are you often a loser? Do you easily get sidelined?

Sometimes we expect others to read our minds: they should know what we are thinking and what we want. But how can they unless they are telepathic? Try telling people what you need (a cuddle, help with the shopping, extra time to meet a deadline); give others the chance to be thoughtful.

Your Child Within

What has happened to that irrepressible energy and the fascination with the world that you had as a child? How come it all looks so ordinary now? Where did that child-like wonder go?

Your child is still within you, full of delight and brimming with mischief and excitement. Get in touch with your inner child and bring some sparkle back into your life.

- Admire a photograph of the baby you.
- Blow bubbles, eat candy floss, ride on a donkey ... enjoy childish fun!
- Look at life through the eyes of a child. How wonderful it is!

Stop Gossiping

If we are critical and judgemental about other people, we actually change the way we feel about ourselves.

How do you feel about a person who gossips about others?

Could you trust a person like that?

Could they ever be a close friend of yours?

The next time you find yourself about to criticise someone, ask yourself if you really need to do this. Will it change anything for the better? If it won't, then stop.

If you always look for something positive to say about others, you will find that everyone will feel more energised and upbeat (including you).

Just Smile!

It's a bad day; you are feeling unhappy, depressed, sad ... You are looking low and you feel as if you can't communicate with others. Other people back off and so the negative feelings increase.

Yet a smile can often break a negative cycle of:

- Feeling down.
- Looking fed-up.
- Other people not bothering to communicate with you.
- Increased depression ('You see, I'm so worthless no one likes me ...')

SMILE! (Eyes as well!) Fake it until you make it (this really does work). Adopt the smiling habit – it will take you outside of yourself and help put everything back into perspective.

Your Private Sanctuary

Close your eyes, relax and imagine a beautiful natural scene: the mountains, the seashore, a buttercup meadow ... Whatever you choose, let it feel calm and full of peace.

Now add a shelter (house, cave, healing temple or whatever). Make your shelter a comfortable and safe place. Add the details and look at this wonderful sanctuary you have made. This is your special place and you can come here in the twinkling of an eye; you only have to imagine you are there, and you are!

Come here for rest and spiritual refreshment whenever you feel the need.

Change Your Mind

Always remember that whatever you believe to be true becomes true for you. And you can change your beliefs to transform any area of your life.

- Think of three of your negative self-beliefs and write them down, for example: I never get things right.

- Change these negative thoughts by making contradictory positive statements, for example: I always do the best I can.

- Contradict all your negative beliefs (what good are they doing you?) and you will become more upbeat, interesting and confident.

Decide to change your mind. You are a unique and amazing person. Live like one!

A Truthful Day

You think you are a truthful person, but let's take a look at today:

- Have you been totally truthful all day?
- Did you really feel 'fine' when you said you did?
- Have you felt angry or sad or anything else and not expressed it?

Do something quite outrageous: tell the truth for a day.

If the truth would hurt just too much ('I hate your new hair colour') then keep it to yourself. But be aware whenever you tell a lie, even by omission.

Tell the truth to yourself and you may discover truths that need to be told.

Give some TLC

Research shows that the more we are able to express ourselves in our environment, the more happy and relaxed we feel.

Give your environment some TLC (Tender Loving Care) and notice the difference it makes to your day.

- Have a bath by candlelight.
- Bring a plant into the office.
- Put fresh flowers in your bedroom.
- Change a room around.
- Light a candle when you have a meal.
- Bring in a photo for your desk at work.
- Play your favourite music when you are doing chores.

Keeping a Calm Centre

Dedicate time to calming your mind and feel the benefits.

- Close your eyes and pay attention to your breathing.

- Become aware of the diaphragm – the muscle in your abdomen that lies below your rib cage. It rises and falls as you breathe.

- Follow its movement with your attention.

- Each time the muscle rises, think 'rising', and every time it falls think, 'falling'.

- Rising ... falling ...rising... falling ... rising ... Let all your other thoughts drift away as you focus on this muscle.

Try this for five minutes a day to start. Keep working at it – it can change your life!

Don't Blame, Just Change

When your relationship is floundering it's so easy to blame your partner, isn't it? But blaming is not a technique that will ever make you feel good. If you get stuck in blame you have given away your power.

Don't blame, just change.

- Use all your incredible inner resources.
- You know what you want and you know how to get it.
- Remember that blame will only get in your way.
- Don't let yourself be a victim.
- Teach your partner to treat you with the respect you deserve.
- Don't ever give away your power.

Keep Bouncing Back

You didn't get the job; a relationship has ended ... And now you are feeling rejected, unappreciated and out of control ...

Don't allow disappointment to wipe out your enthusiasm and confidence (you are bigger than that). Life is all about meeting obstacles, overcoming them and then moving on, so do this!

- Don't lose sight of your dreams.

- Keep focused on your goals.

- Change your attitude and change your approach ('That job wasn't right for me', 'The relationship wasn't working').

- Know that you always have the strength to bounce back and move on.

Attracting Whatever You Radiate

Did you know that energy of a certain type or vibration is inclined to attract energy of a similar quality? This is why grumpy people have miserable lives. You may have thought that they were complaining because their lives are so depressing, but the truth is, their lives are sad because they are grumpy.

Don't try being grumpy for a day – you will have a terrible time. Instead, radiate joy and it will be attracted into your life. Give out warmth and friendship and it will be returned over and over again.

One joyful day may just lead to another.

Dancing to
Your Own Tune

Whose life is this anyway?

- Decide to dance to your own tune.

- List the times when you are not doing what you want.

- Why are you limiting yourself in this way?

- Do you need to stand up for yourself more?

- List ways in which you can do this.

- Be prepared for some people to feel threatened by the new you.

- Take the new assertive you into all areas of your life.

- Remember that this is your life.

Dance to your own tune and the world will dance with you.

A Woman's Gifts

Remind yourself of your brilliance.

- You can do many tasks at once and do them well.
- You are self-aware and intuitive.
- You are visionary as well as practical.
- You are creative and unique.
- You can organise without upsetting others.
- You have a perspective which is different from the male view.
- You are flexible, funny and strong.
- You can express your emotions and encourage your menfolk to do so.
- You know how to make friends.

You are worthy of the deepest admiration and respect. With so much going for you how could you ever doubt yourself?

Mix With Winners

Do you admire your friends and colleagues or are you associating with victims? Some people with low confidence feel threatened by success and choose to spend time with others who are in an even worse state than themselves.

Check your motives.

- Are you friends with that poor helpless person because you are really trying to help her?

- Are you really helping her?

- Does she want to be helped?

- Are you feeling sorry for her?

- Do you feel more confident when you are with her because at least you are more together than she is?

If we choose to spend time with people who cannot handle success we will become just like them.

Failure Leads to Success

The average baby falls over 240 times before she learns to walk. She doesn't give up after the first attempt or even the 239th. No, she keeps picking herself up, dusting herself down and starting all over again until she cracks it.

The human spirit is naturally creative, curious and adventurous. We all want to realise our potential, and if we don't try to be the best we can be, we become depressed and negative.

If you are doing something successfully you have reached its limit. When you are failing and making mistakes you are stepping out into new territory – keep going and embrace your new horizons.

Are You Beating Yourself Up?

If you are busy beating yourself up today (metaphorically speaking), just stop right now. This is not the way forward.

What hook are you hanging yourself on (guilt, self-hate, anger ...?)

- Name your hook and then let yourself off it.
- Self-criticism will lock you into a vicious downward spiral of limitation, depression and supreme negativity.
- Forgive yourself and climb out of your neuroses.

Although this may be hard to believe, I must tell you that:

You are lovable, valuable and wonderful!

How Well-suited Are You?

Use the following assessment to discover just how well you will get along with that new love interest, friend or colleague:

- List four men and four women you admire.
- Reflect upon all the things that you like / love about these people.
- Next to their names make a list of all their positive characteristics (for example, charming, thoughtful, kind, courageous, creative ...)
- Now compare these lists and look for any characteristics that your people have in common.

Use the information you gain to assess your possible compatibility levels with the new people who enter your life.

Letting Go of Blame

Family life is fraught with problems and lurking unre-
solved issues.

As we begin to understand our own negative patterns
we naturally turn to our childhood to discover their
roots. At this point we will probably discover that our
own negative beliefs are closely associated with the
beliefs and behaviour of our parents. The next step is
usually an angry one, as we begin to blame our parents
for what they 'did' to us.

Holding on to blame means holding on to hurt, so just
let go! The more you can forgive, the lighter you will feel.
Give it a try.

Witness Your Life

The witness is the part of you that can observe all your actions, thoughts and feelings. But it never judges you in any way; it takes a purely objective role.

For example, your witness would be aware that you were eating a big cream cake and would only observe this, 'She is eating a big cream cake' (no other emotions would be attached to this).

This ability to distance yourself from your immediate emotions can create a place of inner calm and serenity. Take your witness with you wherever you go and observe yourself in this way (it will really enhance your experiences).

Create Peace of Mind

Try this two-step approach to achieving this wonderful inner state.

Step 1 REMEMBERING PEACEFULNESS

Next time you enjoy a beautiful and peaceful scene, take a mental photograph and commit the view to memory. Collect a 'gallery' of such powerful scenes and memories and replay them whenever you need to tap into feelings of serenity and calm.

Step 2 ACT, DON'T JUST REACT

Peace is a state of mind that we can enter only when we feel in charge of our lives. Victims are always angry with someone and can never feel truly centred and calm. Be assertive and be active instead of reactive.

Feel Free

As partners, parents, colleagues and family members, we can be pulled in many directions. Sometimes the responsibilities of life can grind us down until we feel cut off from our own needs, dreams, passions and goals.

How often have you not done something because it would mean putting your own needs before someone else's?

See yourself standing tall and alone in a beautiful and deserted landscape; this world is yours for the taking.

Know that you are always free to be yourself and to follow your dreams.

Be Brave For a Day

Do you ever find yourself saying or thinking, 'I'd love to ... but I couldn't possibly do it'? Most of our dreams and desires remain unfulfilled not because we tried and failed but because we never tried at all.

What is it that you would love to do but haven't? Why haven't you?

- Take this day and live it bravely: say what you think, do what you want and take the risk.
- Be realistic: what is the worst thing that can happen to you?
- Be courageous and let your brave day become a brave tomorrow.

Yes, you can do this!

Surf the Alpha Waves

For most of the day our brains are operating on the beta wavelength (logical, rational, thinking mind).

Alpha waves are relaxing, calming and creative. One way to tap into them is by slowing your breathing.

- Check how many breaths you take in a minute.

- By reducing this number to nine or less you will feel calmer, relaxed and in control.

- Become aware of your breathing and make it as slow and deep as you can.

As your breathing slows down, your thought patterns also slow down. You will feel refreshed and revitalised when you return to beta mode.

Being a Winner

- Change any negative thoughts about yourself and replace them with this positive thought: 'I am doing the best I can'.

- Visualise success. Imagine a scene where your dreams come true. Repeat your visualisation frequently.

- Believe in yourself and always follow through your decisions.

- Smile. Within ten seconds of smiling your body is flooded with feel-good chemicals. Use your smile to lift the mood at that important interview / meeting / date – it will make a difference.

- Keep confident and trust your decision-making powers.

A Natural Creative

You are a one-off, utterly unique and totally original, and this is how you entered the world. But many of your natural creative gifts may have been lost or buried in your childhood.

Check to see if you have any negative beliefs and ideas that may be limiting your creativity.

- Was your creativity encouraged or curtailed?

- Did you get to do whatever you were longing to do, or were you often disappointed?

- Were you ever encouraged to display your natural talents or were you steered into the mainstream?

You are a natural creative. So create!

Are You Moving Too Fast?

Planning, time management and list writing may help to keep our lives in order but they are not the only life skills we need.

If you are so organised that you live in the future then you are missing the true pleasure of the moment. Next time you catch yourself speeding ahead and feeling stretched, say to yourself, 'Be here now' and just take some time out to take stock of your situation.

Nothing is ever so important that it can't wait a second for you to centre yourself. Slow down and stop trying to be Superwoman (or man).

Money Can't Buy It

It's so easy to believe that our lives would be more meaningful if only we were rich, famous and successful. But a fairy-tale mansion full of designer goodies would not necessarily make us feel good about ourselves.

- Are you low or high in self-esteem?
- Do you value and respect yourself?

Without self-worth our whole life becomes meaningless and chaotic. If we bring ourselves down others will soon agree with us that we are 'not good enough', 'useless', etc. And we can't buy self-esteem, however rich we are, because it is an inner quality based on positive self-belief.

Value and respect yourself; self-worth comes from within.

Stay Super-young

Do you believe that we lose brain cells as we age?

Studies show that this isn't actually true and that people in their sixties and seventies experience a decrease in mental capacity of less than 1 per cent annually (rising to 2 per cent in their eighties).

A recent psychological study of the super-young (people who look, feel and behave decades younger than their age) highlights the key components of their youthful mental vigour.

The Super-young:

- Think for themselves and are open to originality
- Don't criticise themselves
- Often keep working beyond retirement age
- Are adaptable and flexible
- Have a playful mental attitude

One-minute Holiday

- Sit down in a quiet place and close your eyes.

- Become aware of your breathing and start to feel deeply relaxed.

- In your mind's eye begin to create a beautiful scene. You can choose any outdoor setting you wish: the beach, the mountains, a garden, a tropical island ...

- Fill the scene with colour and detail. See the sights; smell the fragrances; hear the birdsong, the running water, the waves crashing on the rocks.

- When you have created your ideal holiday spot, you can gently return to reality.

Now you can just close your eyes at any time and be there!

Mirror Work

Look in the mirror, look deeply into your own eyes and tell yourself how much you love and value yourself. You might use your name:

I (name) love and value myself.

Repeat this and watch yourself carefully. Make this exercise as meaningful as possible. This is really the most powerful way of making affirmations and it can be very confronting. If this is too hard then write your affirmations until it becomes easier for you to work with the mirror.

Mirror work moves energy fast. If self-change is your goal, then persevere with this technique.

What Are You Carrying Around With You?

There is no doubt that positive self-beliefs create dramatic changes in our lives: we increase our self-esteem and self-respect, and others mirror those beliefs.

If we believe that we are capable, creative and interesting, then other people will believe it too! We 'carry' our personal qualities in our aura, and others respond to our energy field. So watch what you are 'carrying' around with you.

- Respect yourself and others will respect you.

- Trust yourself and others will trust you.

- Believe in the goodness of life and you will attract the good.

Hot Sex

Is your sex life sizzling?

A hectic lifestyle in which we are often juggling career, home and family life can lead to no time or energy for sex. Without some creative touches sex can easily become a boring routine.

Try the following:

- Share your fantasies.
- Use candlelight.
- Sip champagne in bed.
- Buy some sexy clothes.
- Think up some surprises.
- Burn scented oils.
- Give each other a massage.
- Experiment!

The Magic of Positive Energy

✫

When relationships are in a rut our energy gets stuck in a negative downward spiral. If anyone gives us a compliment when we are feeling like this, we are likely not only to disbelieve them but also to spoil the moment for them.

Think of this in energetic terms. You give someone positive energy (a compliment of some sort) and they can't accept it. What a waste of good energy! How flat we feel.

Positive energy brings magic and power with it, but it must be allowed into our life for it to work.

Learn to take compliments gracefully and enjoy!

Stop Nagging Yourself

Whenever our confidence is low we become our own worst enemy. Who needs enemies when we are so good at beating ourselves up? We know exactly the most painful points to make and so down we go into a familiar negative spiral of our very own making.

You can break this pattern by forgiving yourself.

- What did you do that was really so bad that you must punish yourself forever and ruin your life?
- Haven't you blamed yourself enough?
- Does continual self-blame achieve anything useful?

Step out of those nagging shoes, lighten up and move on towards your true potential.

Let Go of Your Guilt

Guilt destroys self-esteem, stops all progress and can keep you awake at night.

How often have you found yourself wracked by guilt, flying from pillar to post, trying to be all things to all people, always in a no-win situation and with your self-esteem dropping through the floor?

- Guilt is like a rusty old hook in the ceiling, and when you let yourself hang on it there is no way out.

- Whenever guilt attacks, just visualise it floating away in a bubble, never to darken your doorway again.

- Let go of guilt and let yourself off that hook.

Live in Harmony

Life throws us all together in a great melting pot, and we can find ourselves in many potentially difficult situations: working with people we don't like; having to spend time with relatives who rub us up the wrong way; facing stressful situations, losing our cool, and feeling criticised and misunderstood.

We human beings are here to learn to live and to work together, and whenever we achieve this in some way we feel really great (for example, we reach a team target at work, or our relations come together to celebrate a family event).

Learn to tolerate differences and strive for harmony – it really is worth it.

Recharge Your Batteries

Try this in any spare moment in your working day and feel the difference in your energy.

- Lie down on your back. Rest your upper arms on the floor and your hands on your abdomen.

- Use a small cushion to support your head.

- Pull up your legs with your knees pointing to the ceiling. Keep your feet flat on the floor and your knees apart. As you do this you will feel your lower back moving closer to the floor. Rest in this position for a few minutes.

Push up your energy and productivity levels by recharging your batteries throughout the day.

More Tips for a Positive Self-image

- Use assertive body language. Walk tall and carry yourself with pride and you will feel so much better about yourself.

- Smile and the world smiles with you. Laugh more and you will look and feel great.

- Keep your energy levels high by making sure you eat well and take enough exercise. When your energy is buzzing and positive you look and feel wonderful.

- A positive self-image attracts attention. Become an exciting and interesting person who radiates confidence and knows that they are so much more than their size and shape.

At the Crossroads

- Feeling stuck, fed-up, bored?
- Feel that life is just a dull routine?
- Is work getting you down?
- Is your relationship in a rut?
- Any other complaints?

If you answered 'yes' to any of these questions, you are standing at a crossroads in your life and it's time to make a change. It may look as if your life is just happening to you and you have no control, but this isn't true. If you act like a victim you will be treated like one.

If you want to change just start with yourself, the rest will follow.

A Heavy Head?

With the average head weighing in at about a stone and with the weight of our pressing thoughts on top of this, it surely is some miracle that we can keep our heads upright for so many hours each day!

You are so much more than your mind: you are mind, body and spirit. Sometimes it seems that we are so busy thinking things (with our mind) and doing things (with our body) that we can never truly relax and let go.

Stop doing and thinking for a moment and just be. Let your natural spirituality shine through.

You Can Survive

Seven tips to survive (whoever life throws at you):

1 Always try to bring out the best in people.

2 Expect others to treat you well.

3 Respect yourself – and others will feel respect for you.

4 Create some personal boundaries for yourself.

5 Be tolerant of the shortcoming of others.

6 Use good communication skills. Be a good listener. This makes people feel that you really care about them.

7 Say what you mean clearly. Be straightforward. People will appreciate knowing where they stand with you.

Always try to overcome discord: people matter!

Slow time

Are you flying around doing it all and having it all? Are you becoming a do-aholic? When we live like this our work becomes a burden, and creative and inspirational energy go underground.

Slow down. Pencil in some slow time if that's the only way you can get around to it. And then try the following:

1 Turn off the TV.
2 Learn a simple relaxation technique.
3 *Use* the technique.
4 Leave your work at night.
5 Have a real weekend (switch your answermachine on).

The world won't come to a stop if you do.

— 8 —

Colour Healing

We all respond to colour, and scientists have discovered that each colour sends a unique message to the brain which affects our moods in different ways.

Look at the list below and think about how the colour of your clothes and décor can enhance particular moods.

- RED is physically stimulating.

- YELLOW is good for increasing optimism.

- ORANGE boosts security – also wear it to lift your love life!

- GREEN represents natural healing and balance.

- PINK attracts TLC (tender loving care).

- BLUE is good for when you want to appear cool.

- PURPLE increases spiritual awareness.

Do What You Came to Do

What is your personal mission statement?

In other words, what is your life's purpose – why exactly are you here? To make the world a happier place? To make people laugh? To raise public awareness of environmental issues? To ensure that your children have high self-esteem? To spread positivity and hope? To teach, listen and respond?

When you can make a mission statement, your life will have new direction and purpose. Match your inner drives with real-world activities: do what you came here to do!

Be a Winner

Sports psychology tells us that winning has as much to do with mental toughness as ability.

Research suggests that up to 70 per cent of our daily thoughts are negative as opposed to positive (on a bad day there must be an even higher percentage of negatives). But we have the power to change this! We can use our mental ability to create winning situations in our everyday life.

Today remind yourself that:

- Anything in life is possible: whenever you think that you can't, know that you can.

- Winning is not always about being first, it is about always giving your best and striving to reach your potential.

Listen Well Today

Instead of focusing on talking, focus on listening: spend today listening to everyone you meet rather than talking to them. Of course you will have to speak, but keep all chat to the bare minimum.

It's so easy to forget to listen and to be rushing ahead in our thoughts, planning what we are going to say next.

Active listening shows that we value and understand what the other person is communicating. When we can show others that we respect their input, they feel validated and appreciated.

When we listen well, everybody wins and relationships blossom.

Your Family Gallery

Each of us is part of something so much bigger, and our families show us this. Keep turning up for family gatherings and know that these people are important to you.

Capture the essence of your family gatherings by taking lots of photos and create a gallery in your home. Devote a wall to family snaps and keep changing them around as you take new ones. When I'm writing I often look up at my gallery to see my father, or one of my sons, or my daughter, husband, mother, granddaughter, brother ... looking out at me, and they always give me a strong sense of purpose and continuity.

No Regrets

Do you ever lie awake at night worrying and blaming yourself for past actions?

Do you ever wish that you hadn't done something, had acted differently or made some other response?

Life is too short both to stuff a mushroom and to have regrets! We cannot change the past so why not just change direction and look to a brighter future.

Recriminations are draining and take away the joy of living. We always do the best we can at the time. So give yourself a break and use your positive energy to create new directions and possibilities.

A Hassle-free Future

Because we are all unique we react differently to situations. One person's stress motivator ('I can meet that tight deadline') is another person's stress poison ('Oh no, it's too much pressure for me').

Recognise what presses your stress buttons.

- Identify all unnecessary stress in your life. Make a list.
- Reflect upon each item on your list. Ask yourself whether you can let go of it, change it or accept it.
- Write one of these three options next to each stress item.

Now do what is necessary. Changing your approach to life will change your life!

— 15 —

Life Is Short

As a member of the '24-hour society' you may well suffer from the following uncomfortable symptoms:

- Feeling rushed, pressurised and stressed.
- Stiff shoulders, tension headaches.
- Inability to relax completely.
- Feeling irritable and forgetful.
- Having difficulty making decisions.

This non-stop lifestyle, which lets us buy anything and do anything at any time of day or night, means that we are finding it harder and harder to know when to stop. The pressure is on and we are feeling it!

Schedule time for yourself. Stop or you will drop. Life is short – make the most of it!

Increase Your Personal Power

When we are high in personal power we are:

Energetic–Enthusiastic–Motivated–Flexible–Happy
–High in self-worth–Creative–Decisive–Focused

How often do you feel like this?

To be high in personal power we must be ready to take complete responsibility for everything that happens to us. Stop blaming and take charge of your life. Start by taking the following three important steps:

Step1 Say 'no' when you need to.

Step2 Express your true feelings.

Step3 Don't ever act like a victim.

Stop blaming and start living dynamically. You have it in you!

Six Tips for a Positive Self-image

- Stop comparison shopping. When you compare yourself with others you will always feel intimidated.

- Love and appreciate all that your body does for you. You are perfect just the way you are.

- Celebrate your unique qualities and optimise your best features.

- Always be yourself; never try to be someone else.

- Look beyond the image in the mirror and see the talented and creative person that you are.

- You can enjoy the fantasy of glossy media hype but don't let impossible dreams steal your happiness.

Life Zone Quiz

Relationships: Do your relationships support you? Do you ever feel taken for granted?

Self-Image: Are you positive and upbeat? Do you believe in yourself?

Health and Fitness: Does your lifestyle support good health? Are you high in body confidence?

Money: Are you good at managing your money? Do you ever spend more than you earn?

Work: Do you like your work? Would you like a career change?

Spirituality: Are you able to switch off from doing and just be? Can you tap into your inner strength?

What action do you need to take? Take it!

A Natural Break

I speak to many people who struggle to keep confident, happy and calm and who frequently feel unable to maintain a positive outlook. Often these problems are related to lifestyle conditions. Some simple changes can often transform a negative state of mind.

If you can't remember what colour the grass is you need to take a natural break.

- Bring some plants and flowers into your workplace.

- Get out for a walk at lunchtime (somewhere green if possible).

- Consciously slow down and appreciate the colour of the sky, the sounds of birds, the smell of a flower.

Finding the Balance

Tips for balancing work and home:

1 Prioritise yourself! Schedule free time for doing nothing, even if you are surrounded by chaos.

2 Learn to settle for a less than perfect home. Domestic jobs just keep on coming. Accept this and stop trying to always keep on top.

3 Delegate household tasks. Make a list of jobs for everyone and make sure they do them. This is as easy as it sounds (I've done it and it works a treat).

4 Leave your work thoughts at work.

5 Leave your home thoughts at home.

An Angelic Blessing

Transfer the words below onto paper or card to make your own set of Angelic Blessing Cards.

These cards provide key words that will help you to focus on particular aspects of your inner life.

SIMPLICITY	INSPIRATION	HEALING
SPONTANEITY	COURAGE	TRUTH
BEAUTY	HARMONY	CREATIVITY
COMPASSION	FORGIVENESS	TENDERNESS
FAITH	UNDERSTANDING	FREEDOM
LOVE	INTEGRITY	BALANCE

Lay out your cards face downwards in front of you. Focus on a problem and ask for divine assistance. Choose a card and reflect on its meaning. Absorb the qualities that this blessing brings.

Strengthen your divine connection and amazing things will start to happen.

— 22 —

Feeling blue?

- Make contact with someone you love. Write a letter, send an email, phone a friend, give someone a hug ... Give your love, with no strings attached, and you will feel great.
- Create something – a cake, a meal, a tidy room. Light a candle, put a bunch of flowers on the table. Give the project (however small) all of your attention. Admire the results: you can and do make a difference.

Someone once said that we are here to learn how to live and not how to win. Feel glad, just to be alive.

How to Brighten Your Day

How enthusiastic are you feeling today, on an scale from 1 (non-existent) to 10 (buzzing with it)?

Enthusiasm is a powerful force that attracts positive attention and really gets things moving, but sometimes it can be hard to feel enthused. Try the following to lift your mood:

- Be committed to whatever task is at hand and your interest levels will soar.

- Perform an act of kindness and do it anonymously; you will be surprised how this makes you feel.

- Act as if you are enthusiastic and you will start to feel it.

Life is a boomerang: whatever you give out comes back to you.

Keep Your Relationship Sparkling

Whatever happens to the romance you feel at the start of a new love affair? When heart-stopping affairs turn into long-term relationships, things often change.

Ways to keep being romantic:

- Keep talking to each other about how you feel, the ups and downs of your days. Listen as well as talk, and you will find that your emotional sharing creates a close bond that increases sexual desire.

- Remember that bad sex is hardly ever about technique and nearly always about lack of close communication.

Share your deepest feelings and thoughts and feel that sparkle return.

Family Power

Family occasions always create a mixture of emotions. As we connect with the ones who share our genetic heritage we feel our biological and ancestral roots and we acknowledge where we come from.

But running alongside the strength of our blood ties is also the recognition of shared patterns and beliefs. It's true to say that the things that annoy and irritate us most about our family members are often the traits we share with them.

Keep connecting with your family. We all need to feel our shared roots (even if we do sometimes get cross with each other!).

Be Decisive

Are you decisive?

Yes / no / can't decide?

On a bad day, when your confidence levels are low and you are feeling vulnerable, it can be very hard to trust your own judgement. We all know what this feels like: Is it a good idea? ... Perhaps it is ... On the other hand maybe it isn't ... Get back on track by taking the following three steps:

1 Ask yourself exactly what you want to happen; clarify your outcome.

2 Decide what behaviour you will need to change in order to achieve your goal.

3 ACT. Just do it. Do not give yourself time to hesitate.

Love in Action

Happiness, inspiration, meaning and purpose are what really shape our understanding and enrich our lives.

And our experiences become truly amazing when we can share them with others. Remember that everyone is connected at a very deep level and we all want to be understood and appreciated by other people.

Value and treasure the ones who make your day so good. This means actually doing something to show your deep appreciation (think of this as love in action).

Take your good relationships one step further and actively show your love for the people you value in your life.

Reduce Your Sensitivity

Find somewhere quiet to sit and relax.

- Imagine a beautiful bubble in front of you.

- Notice its colour.

- It starts to grow in size and beauty until it is bigger than you.

- Step into your radiant bubble.

- You now feel totally protected.

- You know that nothing and no one can harm you when you are inside your beautiful bubble.

Use this brilliant technique whenever you are feeling exposed, vulnerable or sensitive to others. You can do this anywhere at any time (even in that pressurised work meeting).

Life's Lessons

Life is here to teach us. We are here to make mistakes, learn from our lessons and so evolve our consciousness.

But when we are low in self-esteem we believe that we are our mistakes.

When you feel like this remember the following:

- We all make mistakes.
- We learn by encouragement and not by criticism.
- Never kick yourself when you are down.
- If you have to, just pick yourself up, dust yourself down and start all over again.
- You can and will bounce back.

You are much bigger than your mistakes.

The Emotion Cooler

Use the Emotion Cooler whenever you are nervous, upset or angry.

- Place your right thumb over your right nostril, lightly closing it off.

- Exhale completely.

- Slowly inhale and exhale through your left nostril only for 20 complete breaths. Keep your mouth closed throughout.

- Make the breaths long and smooth.

- Every time you breathe out, let go of all your negative emotions. Visualise the hurt, tension and anger leaving you as you exhale.

Don't wait to feel stressed before you do this exercise; it will always improve any mood and leave you feeling clear, relaxed and positive.

Your Core Values

What does success mean to you?

Are you looking for promotion, security, excitement, peace of mind, a high profile career, a creative outlet ...?

Now, think about the personal values that are most important to you. One way to discover these values is to think of the character traits that you most admire and value in other people. Make a list of them. For example, enthusiasm, humility, kindness, honesty, patience, drive, positivity, creativity, humour ...

If you want to feel successful you must know your core values and be able to integrate them into your personal and working life.

— 2 —

More Quality Time

Enhance your life.

Think about quality rather than quantity. Quality time is spent doing things that you love to do. What are those things that you would love to make time for? Evaluate your lifestyle and check out how you use your precious time.

- List the way you use your time throughout the week.
- Make another list of the activities that bring you most fulfilment.
- Now compare your lists.
- Look for the differences between your lists.
- How could you rearrange things to allow for even greater personal satisfaction?

Do it!

Go With the Flow

Whenever you are truly inspired by something – a piece of music, a beautiful rose, a new project, a workout at the gym, an exciting new relationship – your spiritual energy is at work, uplifting, harmonising, expanding, calming and centring you. The word 'inspire' is linked with the word 'spirit'; your spiritual energy is light and free because it is connected to the universal energy flow.

- Go with the flow and feel the difference.
- When you go with the flow everything falls into place.
- Go with the tide rather than against it and you will always know which step to take.

Heart Thoughts

Living in a consumer society often leads us to think that having more things, more money, and bigger and better cars and houses will bring us great happiness and fulfilment.

But although the material world offers all sorts of enticements, it cannot open our hearts to each other. Things are only things, and what really matters to people is the heart.

- Spending time with someone is the best gift you can give.
- Let people know that you are thinking of them and they will be touched.
- All the best things in life are free.

A Dirty Word

We often associate the word 'no' with behaviour that is described as thoughtless, mean, hard, uncaring, etc.

Whenever you are afraid to say 'no' just take away this emotional content and see the real meaning of your communication.

- When I say 'no' to you it only means that I don't want to do what you are asking of me. It does not mean that I am rejecting you as a person.

- When you say 'no' to me it simply means that you don't want to do what I'm asking. It does not mean that you are personally rejecting me.

'No' is not a dirty word.

Reframing a Situation

- Think of any personal situation that can be a problem for you (it can bring about stressful feelings).

- Visualise this problem in glorious Technicolor. Look at it as if you are watching a movie.

- Now drain the colour, sound and action from the picture. Shrink it until it disappears completely.

- Replace it with a new, bright and positive image in which all your problems have been resolved. Hear the new sounds, see the new action and feel your calm emotions.

Reframing is a great way to get to grips with potential stressors before they get to grips with you!

Do It Badly

Have you ever not bothered even to start a creative project because you know that you will fail to be as brilliant as you want to be?

Remember that there are no overnight sensations. Brilliant work comes from 1 per cent inspiration and 99 per cent dedication. This is such a good thing to remember. You need the inspiration only to begin; the rest is all about perseverance and putting in the hours. And the perseverance part involves the creator (at some point) doing the painting / acting / writing / whatever badly.

Do it badly or don't do it at all!

Good work follows bad. Keep going!

8

Be Here Now

If you get so organised that you are always planning the future or you are rushing to keep track of time, then things are getting out of control.

Stop a moment and remind yourself to become aware of the moment – be here now.

The power is always in the moment. Stop reading and recognise this very moment. Feel the now.

'Later' doesn't really exist because we are only ever conscious in the present moment. 'Later' always lies in the future.

- Feel the now.
- Appreciate this precious moment of your life.

Stay consciously with the moment, every moment.

Sexual Confidence

Sexy images surround us; everywhere we look we see gorgeous young things radiating glamour and sexuality. The pressure is on to be a sex goddess / god as well as a partner / worker / kitchen wizard / parent ... How is it possible to be all these things?

If you don't come in from work feeling glamorous, sexy and ready for a night of love, just relax. The reality is that we all struggle with our self-image and sexual confidence. The key to is to create a positive self-image.

Sexual confidence is not dependent on how look on the outside; it is all about how you feel on the inside.

You Are in Charge

Your life doesn't have to be a chaotic muddle from the moment you wake up to the moment you collapse into bed. You don't have to run an obstacle race every day; you can take charge.

And this doesn't mean sticking to rigid rules and time schedules and turning your life into a military manoeuvre. You can relax and take control!

- Check your life zones: Relationship, Self-image, Fitness; Money, Work and Spirituality.
- Are any of them out of balance?
- Decide what needs changing and change it.

Make your life work for you and you will feel in control.

A Natural High

There is no doubt that fresh air, sunshine, birdsong and the proximity of growing things are great soothers for a troubled mind. We may search for peace and tranquillity in pills, books, chocolate cake, relationships, alcohol, shopping, etc. (add your own specials to this list), but we know that all these things do not work, at least not for long. Our state of mind can be improved so easily by simply getting in touch with the rhythms of the natural world.

So escape the town for a few hours each week. If this isn't possible, find a park. Take a good book, a picnic and enjoy!

Using Your Intuitive Powers

- Think of three times when you followed your intuition and things turned out well.

- Now think of three things that your intuitive voice has been urging you to do. These can be small things, for example: reply to that letter, read that book, contact that friend, or they may be larger matters such as: go for a new job, give up that man, make some lifestyle changes.

- Now ask yourself why you haven't done them.

You see you do know what's going on; that inner voice of yours keeps sending you messages to help you keep on track.

Listen to it!

Doing It All

The pressure of having to keep it all together can turn us into speed freaks who can't even stop to take a breath as we rush from pillar to post throwing and catching all those balls.

If this sounds like you, it's time to reassess your lifestyle and change your outlook. You can only give what you have, and if your goodwill and energy run out, everything comes to a standstill. If you burn out, the game is over.

- Don't put yourself at risk.
- Always put your health and well-being first.
- Create a more balanced lifestyle.

Start immediately!

A Slimmer, Healthier You

What you eat today becomes what you are tomorrow. Our health and well-being can depend upon what we consume.

- Wean yourself off processed and refined foods.
- Drink at least six glasses of water a day (mineral or filtered).
- Walk a mile or two as often as possible.
- Cut down on alcohol.
- Be aware of your posture – walk tall, shoulders back and stomach in (you will look at least 2 kg slimmer).

Look For Beauty

Sometimes we are so busy keeping it all together that we lose sight of the miraculous wonder of life.

Today put on your appreciative eyes and go out and look for something to cherish. Keep looking until you feel your heartstrings tug. Some things you could look for are: small flowers growing in pavement cracks, a smile from a stranger, a bird singing just for the joy of it, any act of kindness ... Leave your judgements behind, look for beauty and you will find it.

Do it again tomorrow.

Re-invent Yourself

Feeling stuck and bored? Why not change your perspective by re-inventing yourself and trying out something new? Do something out of character and see things in a new way (it's a great way to push up confidence levels).

Here are a few ideas to be going on with:

- Change your dress style / hair style.
- Start a new hobby.
- If you like rock, why not try the opera?
- If you always wear black, go for primary colours.

Change is fun. It's like a breath of fresh air flowing into your life!

Work and Home

More tips for balancing work and home:

1 Book some exercise time into your diary, but don't take your foreign language tapes with you to the gym (practise doing one thing at a time).

2 Slow down: your breathing, your talking, your pace. Take time to appreciate your life.

3 Look at the bigger picture: you are meant for greater things than meeting all those targets.

4 Take time to stand and stare; practise this and you will find the habit will grow on you.

5 When you just can't beat the clock remember your sense of humour. Laughter helps bring things back into perspective.

Go On a Date (With Yourself)

A great tip and a wonderful excuse to please yourself.

Take yourself somewhere you would love to go: an art gallery, a shop where you can buy something special, the river, the theatre, a health club ... the choice is yours, but I'm sure you get the idea.

Plan your date with yourself (what you will wear, when you will go) as if you were going out with someone who is very important to you. And of course you are going with an important person: your relationship with yourself is the most important one that you will ever have.

Being Your Higher Self

Your Higher Self is the part of you that connects with the universal power source: it connects you spiritually.

It can transcend the minutiae of life and is able to see the larger perspective.

It speaks to you through your intuition and flashes of insight.

Become your Higher Self and become aware of the Higher Selves of everyone you meet. Know that we all have a wise and knowing Self that gives us faith, endurance, compassion and kindness. Reach for the highest truth you have and strive to see the best in others – we are all spiritual beings.

Be a First-rate Version of Yourself

It's an important occasion and you want to look and sound fabulous, but the adrenaline is coursing through your veins and you feel nerve-wracked.

What to do?

- Take some long, deep breaths and decide just to be yourself. Others know when we are putting on airs and graces and it always signals our insecurities.

- The best impression you can make is the one you create when you are being natural.

- Always be a first-rate version of yourself rather than a second-rate version of someone else.

— 21 —

Get a Grip on Stress

Nothing is actually intrinsically stressful. This is so hard to believe when we are feeling tense and uptight, but possible to acknowledge when we are feeling relaxed and happy.

Stress lies in the eye of the beholder: if we see a situation or person as threatening then we will register stress.

- Check out the things that make you stressed.
- Why do they affect you so badly?
- What can you do to limit their effect?
- Are you standing up for yourself?
- Do you need to make some changes?

Get Moving

Escape from all your pressures; just get out there and run / cycle / walk ...

You will:

- Increase your oxygen uptake and your feel-good endorphin levels.
- Use up calories (always a plus).
- Tone your muscles.
- Give your logical, rational, linear, left brain a rest.
- Come back feeling happier, more creative and inspired, more more alert and productive, and with a better sense of perspective.

Sometimes we do need to take time to work things out, but the best way to do this is by keeping our creative energy upbeat and positive.

What Gets You Going?

What happens to you when you are feeling stressed? How do you react? Do you get angry, yell a lot, withdraw, get a headache, feel exhausted, eat chocolate or sticky buns? And what causes you to feel stressed?

Keep a stress diary for a week:

- Note what causes and triggers your feelings of stress.

- Where and when does it most happen?

- List your feelings. Do you become depressed, irritable, frantic, tired?

- And then how do you react?

Get acquainted with your own stress personality and you can learn to stop your stress reaction before it starts.

Order Out of Chaos

Appreciate your home:

- Clear away the clutter and you will find that your mind will be clearer. Just try to keep your own bedroom orderly if the rest is too much.

- Plants lift the atmosphere, so place them around your home.

- Play uplifting music as you do domestic chores – it adds grace and lightness to the work.

- Don't ever do housework in a resentful frame of mind – it will make the burden very heavy.

- Eat by candlelight: bring some romance to the dinner table.

- Appreciate your home: it is your castle.

Men Will Be Men

What single thing would most improve the quality of your life?

A recent survey by a women's magazine reveals that 60 per cent of women answering this question asked only that their partner would spend just 15 minutes a day talking to them 'meaningfully'.

Men speak an average of 12,000 words a day, while women average 23,000 words. No surprises here. And some of us might even consider 12,000 to be rather an optimistic figure!

Don't expect too much of your man.

Men and women communicate differently!

Men speak to give information and women speak to create emotional bonds.

You Can Do This

Our personal levels of self-esteem depend entirely on the power of our self-belief. Everyone has self-esteem issues because we are all always working towards greater self-awareness.

When you next find yourself looking low self-esteem in the eye, just remember that you can always change your reponses; you don't have to go down that well-worn path of negativity.

Our habitual patterns have been learned and they can be unlearned.

Get out of the self-blame game and stop punishing yourself.

Let yourself off these self-defeating hooks and nurture your positive self-belief.

You can do this; you only need to think you can!

The Wise Person Within

Just believe for a moment that you have access to all the answers to your problems.

Close your eyes and imagine that there is a wise all-knowing person inside you and that she can give you help whenever you need it.

Now open your eyes and you can stop imagining, because you really do possess this inner wisdom, you only need to use it! Are you struggling with this idea? Is it hard to accept that you have extraordinary intuitive powers?

Ask for guidance from the wise person within and you will receive it. Just try this and see!

Letting Go of Addictions

Write down your answers to this exercise:

1 Describe your relationship with your addiction.

2 What don't you like about your condition?

3 How do you want things to change? Be specific.

4 Recognise why you have become addicted. Deep self-hatred, the need to fill the emptiness inside, fear of anger, lack of trust, desire to be in control, a need to punish yourself and lack of self-forgiveness are some of the things that may have brought you here.

5 Seek help. Find a counsellor or a support group that can help you.

You are bigger than any addiction!

Positive Parents

Bringing up children is a wonderful but totally demanding experience.

Disciplining is a sensitive issue, and the way we do it will affect the quality of our relationship with our child. We are not taught to be parents; we have to learn the skills on the job.

However, there are some strategies that can help to smooth our way.

- Set rules and explain what will happen if they are broken.

- Be consistent.

- Give your time – so that bad behaviour is not the only way of getting attention.

- Look for the positive. Praise and cuddles for trying hard are much more effective than punishment.

Love Is All You Need

There are only two ways of looking at the world: through the eyes of fear or the eyes of love. Choose the framework of love and positivity and open your heart to embrace compassion, understanding and awareness.

Did you know that your heart will open if you:

- Find something to appreciate,
- Tell someone how much they mean to you.
- Look into a mirror and say to yourself, 'I am good enough, just the way I am.'
- Forgive someone. This is absolutely guaranteed to make you feel amazing!

Enjoy this Perfect Moment

As the search for de-stressing therapies increases, we are offered a myriad ways to become calm, centred and at peace. Treatments, gadgets, techniques, courses, supplements, books, workshops ... a never-ending list of feel-good strategies to help us simplify our complicated lives.

But no amount of money can buy peace and tranquillity because these qualities lie within you. So, wherever you are today:

- Stop for a few seconds and take a look around you.

- Appreciate this perfect moment of your life.

- Become aware of your breathing as you take in the life force and fill yourself with energy.

Be Approachable

We are drawn to people who look on the bright side of life, whose energy is attractive and friendly, who don't bore us with their fixed opinions, and who know how to be flexible and how to ease the tension within a group. Such people are popular because they are fun to be with.

When things get heavy:

- Lighten up the situation with laughter and humour.

- Suspend all judgements about how things or people 'should' be.

- Take a broader view, enjoy a higher perspective and you will feel clearer and be more approachable.

— 2 —

Let Your Light Shine

We are usually so involved in earthly matters – making money, looking after the kids, keeping our relationship together, getting our career on track – that we often don't have any time or space to think about spiritual matters.

Make time to develop your spiritual connection:

- See the bigger picture.
- Recognise your inner wisdom and act on it.
- Reach for your highest understanding at all times.
- Know that you have amazing inner powers and use them.

Develop your spiritual connection and your life will become richer and more satisfying than you would ever have imagined it could be.

What You Really Want

What do you really really want?

Do you believe that you can go out and get it, or are you standing in the shadows, watching others succeed and feeling like a loser?

- Uncover your hidden desires by noticing any envious thoughts you have about others.

- Become a networker – go out into the world and meet the people whose support you will need.

- Stay focused on your goal but always be prepared to be flexible.

- Visualise your success. See the realisation of your goal in your mind's eye.

- Remember that you are a winner.

Take a Shower of Light

Increase your good feelings. Try the following visualisation to add more clarity and awareness to your mood.

- Imagine a shower of light.
- Step into it and see large drops of white light cascading over you.
- Feel the light energy as it envelops and embraces you.
- See the light turn into the spectrum of rainbow colours.
- Feel the energy of the colours as you absorb them.

Take a shower of light as often as you remember; you will feel uplifted and energised.

De-clutter

When my life is on hold and I feel as if I'm wearing lead boots, it's time to take a trip to the municipal rubbish dump – place of great cleansing and personal catharsis. It's true, I drive away feeling virtuous and pure!

The truth is that when your mind and heart are muddled, then your house (office, desk, car ...) probably is too!

If your life feels stuck, get that energy flowing again by making space. Throw things out to make room for the new. Create a sense of order in your life and your life will feel more ordered!

Be Bold

Our biggest fear is of fear itself – we are afraid of being afraid! And the greatest antidote to this madness is to face our fears with boldness.

Boldness releases powerful forces into the universe and attracts the most amazing responses.

Whenever we act courageously and give it all we've got, our bodies go into emergency standby. This state of emergency unlocks many underused powers that we all possess, including flexibility, commitment, creativity, energy, strength and endurance. You are much more than you think you are!

- Face your fears.
- Think boldly
- Act boldly

Feel strong and powerful.

Perfectionists' Quiz

1 Friends are coming to dinner. Do you have to clean the house, cook a complicated meal and wear yourself out?

2 You are feeling exhausted. Do you carry on regardless?

3 Do you think that you would be happier and more successful if you lost weight?

4 For women: Do you feel incomplete if you aren't wearing make up?

5 Do you sometimes push yourself beyond your limits?

6 Do you like people to think that you are always in control?

7 Do you ever feel that you are not good enough?

Perfectionists are never fulfilled. Let go of these impossible standards.

Getting Men to Talk

You can get your man to talk but you must plan your approach discreetly.

Don't make statements like: You never tell me how you feel or Why don't we talk more? or even Why don't we plan some time to talk? Give the following suggestions a try.

- Organise talk time: create some time in your busy schedules when you can be intimate and attentive. Give him your full attention (men love this).

- Let him talk ... and once he starts chatting, let him talk! Learn to listen well and leave some spaces for him to talk into.

The Wrong Doors

Have ever tormented yourself with such unanswerable questions as:

- Why do I always get the bad luck?

- How come I'm such a loser?

- Why can't someone give me a break?

- When will my life start to take off?

- Why do I always have such lousy relationships?

Such questions lead to the pain of helplessness, frustration and low self-esteem. Is there a question like this that you keep asking yourself over and over again, that tortures you endlessly and doesn't seem to have an answer? Think of such a question as a wrong door for you to go through and stop going through it.

Inner Strength

When the problems pile up we often forget that we have the inner strength and power to overcome any adversity. At times it can feel that life is a maze of difficulties and that we can never find the way out – but we can.

We possess incredible instinctive powers, but we usually fail to use them because we are not taught to value our intuitive gifts.

How many times have you looked back at a situation that has gone badly and thought, I sensed I should have done (this, that or the other); I should have listened to my intuition?

Trust your instincts.

Your Own Amazing Reality

We each create our own reality, and the quality of the life we create depends upon our self-image. Self-critical thoughts always create low self-esteem. How do you see yourself? How does this affect your life?

You can create new and improved realities by visualising and knowing the following:

- You are powerful and strong.
- You can trust yourself.
- You are resourceful and creative.
- You are intelligent and funny.
- Everything you do is a success.

Make your visualisations as clear, bright and detailed as you possibly can. You become your expectations!

Lose Half a Kilogram a Week

Are you feeling overweight, sluggish, fed up with yo-yo dieting?

You only need to have put on a kilo or two to make that gorgeous new outfit totally unwearable.

Here's a tip to help you back into shape – simply.

If you are eating a maintenance diet (that is, you are not putting on weight, just staying the same) you need only to apply the following easy method:

To lose $1/2$ kg a week you need to eat 240 calories less a day and do enough exercise to burn off 350 calories a day (for example, jogging for half an hour).

Life is Precious

Most of us have been touched by tragedy at some time in our lives. When this happens to us, our whole life changes its shape and feels as if it will never be quite the same again. But amidst depression, sadness and perplexity we can always find the true power of the human spirit: people are brave, courageous and amazing!

Misfortune and heartbreak have a way of giving new meaning to our lives by helping us to appreciate every moment.

Human life is such a precious gift and we all have great inner strength. Let this hearten you in times of need.

Stay Away From the Grumpy Gang

To feel upbeat and calm (and remain that way), you need to keep your energy positive.

However brilliant you may be feeling, make sure you stay away from grumpy people; they can and will bring you right down. You may even start to feel guilty about feeling good!

If you recognise this grumpy type of person as someone who is lurking in your life, remember their mission: to make sure that you and everybody else will never have a good day. Stay away from moaners, complainers and cynics, and spend time with positive people; watch your energy and enthusiasm rise!

Silence Is Golden

- Check your diary and lists. Delete unnecessary activities.

- Delegate other duties where possible (for example, create a family rota for household chores).

- With new spaces in your diary you can make appointments with yourself to just do nothing (don't fill the spaces with new activities).

- Spend a few minutes every day in silence. Find some time to be alone even if it has to be before everyone gets up or after they have gone to bed.

- Sit in the silence and enjoy the peace.

- Let this practice become a daily ritual for you and you will be amazed by the positive effects.

Just Enjoy

Happiness and self-belief create harmonious relationships, and harmonious relationships create more
happiness and more self-belief. When you are in the
upward-flowing positive spiral, stay there!

Expecting the best can sometimes be harder to do when
things are going well than when we are struggling with
nothing to lose!

The world is sweet. Accept this and keep expecting it to
be so. Don't start looking for possible problems and
'what ifs'. Just enjoy.

Let your optimist genie out of the bottle. All is well and
you deserve it to be so.

There is no price to pay unless you believe there is.

Relationship Disaster

If your intimate relationships are disaster areas, then check that you are not always falling for the same 'type'.

We are all programmed from childhood to fall for certain types, and by the time we are adolescents our so-called 'love maps' dictate both the personality and physical types of our ideal lovers.

Because these maps can also include hurtful (but comfortably familiar) behaviour from our childhood, you may simply be falling into the trap of unconsciously attracting a lover who is not good for you.

Avoid the attraction trap. Break free from your childhood programming and try someone totally and utterly different.

The Key to Happiness

The key to happiness is appreciation.

Our busy lives often leave us no time just to be ourselves. We may have forgotten the art of just being alive and appreciating the wonder and glory of it all. Simplify and appreciate and your life will be transformed.

- Appreciate your body and all it does for you.
- Focus on what you have rather than on what you don't have.
- Give thanks for the food on your table.
- Value your friendships.
- Look for the beauty in your life and your life will become a beautiful experience.

Walk It Out

One of the most powerful therapies available is absolutely free, almost always possible and appropriate, and it doesn't hurt!

Yes, the act of walking can change your consciousness. You can take your problem for a stroll, come home and things will look different.

Walking is a form of meditation: as we walk our breathing settles into a smooth rhythm, and as our breath lifts and expands, so does our mind.

If you feel as if there is no space left in your head, get walking. Just go! And let your inspiration return to you through your feet.

Be Unique

Do you ever feel that you aren't the same as everyone else, that you don't quite fit in?

Everyone is different! Instead of trying to hide your differences, be creative and make a feature of them.

Look in the places where you feel different; it is here that you will find the keys to your personal and original creativity. So you've got a big nose, wild hair, unusual interests, a shy personality or whatever.

Whenever you feel the urge to fit in, choose to make the most of your differences; they are what make you special, unique and utterly you.

Divine Discontent

It is hard to appreciate our own talents if we feel under-used and lacking in focus. So, if there is gap between the reality of your life and your ambitions, let this be a positive sign for you to change direction.

Be led by your discontent. It will show you:

- What needs to change.
- How to go about the change.

Major clues to self-development are to be found in our (so-called) negativity. Shine a light in your dark places and discover qualities and strengths that you never believed you had.

Stop Being a Martyr

It's time to stop behaving like a martyr and saying 'yes' to all those boring duties that you agreed to (and then wished you hadn't). Martyrdom doesn't give you a saint-like status – it only serves to reduce your self-respect and increase your resentment levels. So stop wasting your valuable time doing things just because others expect you to do them.

Think of one activity that you do reluctantly and ask yourself, 'How can I change things so that I don't waste my time in this way any more?' Be creative about finding ways to extricate yourself from your 'duty' chores and then use your free time to do something for yourself.

Your Wonderful Self

Feel free to be your most wonderful self: enthusiastic, kind, generous, open-hearted, loving and forgiving.

Remember these points:

- When your best is never good enough you have put yourself in a no-win situation.
- If you start confusing what you do with who you are you are slipping into neurotic behaviour.
- Think and speak about yourself positively.
- You can be no more than you believe you are.
- You are more than your mistakes.
- Critical self-beliefs will always keep you down.

You Have the Answers

- When you are troubled and don't know how to act, where do you turn?

- If you can't make a difficult decision, who do you ask?

- When your life is a mess and you need to make changes, how do you start?

- Who is always there for you, in the bad times as well as the good?

- Who knows your weaknesses and strengths and can offer wise counsel at any time of the day or night?

- Who will never let you down?

Look inside – you have all the answers.

Why We Become Addicted

- Every addiction appears to be life-enhancing but is really soul-destroying.

- Addictive behaviour is rooted in self-hate, and an addicted person has low self-esteem.

- If we give away our personal power to others we will always be trying to fill that empty space.

- And this is why so many of us are, or have been, involved in some form of addictive behaviour – to compensate for the lack of fulfilment of our emotional needs.

Low self-worth is at the root of addictive behaviour. Work on your self-esteem if you need to.

Seek help if you need it.

Stop Counting Sheep

Do you crawl reluctantly out of bed in the morning?

Do you need caffeine and carbohydrate pick-me-ups throughout the day?

If so you may be suffering from chronic sleep deprivation.

Tips for a good night's sleep:

- Stick to a regular bedtime – this stabilises your body clock.
- Soak in a warm bath before you go to bed.
- Avoid stimulating drinks a few hours before bedtime (coffee, tea, cola).
- Drink a cup of herbal tea with a sedative effect (try valerian or chamomile).
- Have sex – it relaxes you.
- Ventilate your bedroom.

Make Good Vibrations

The Law of Attraction states that we create whatever we think about. We live within an electromagnetic field and each thought we have charges the energy field with vibrations. Like attracts like. This is the reason why grumpy people really are always having a bad time (negative thought patterns attract all forms of negativity) and upbeat people attract good experiences (positive thought patterns magnetise all forms of positivity).

So 'positive thinking' is more than a fancy self-help term; it is a powerful technique to attract the very best into your life.

Optimism and positivity are fabulous tools – use them!

Ten Important Things
to Remember

1 We are all connected.

2 The more you give, the more you will receive.

3 Love and respect are infinite resources.

4 You create your own reality.

5 Everyone is doing the best they can.

6 Forgiveness (letting go) will accelerate your
   personal development.

7 Every cloud has a silver lining.

8 Your life has meaning and purpose.

9 The universe supports you.

10 You are incredible!

Take time each day to remember at least one of these
things and you will feel the difference.

Be Your Best at Work

More ways to keep assertive at work:

- Let yourself off the hook. Everyone makes mistakes, so when you do, don't bring attention to them. Just let them go and move on.

- Keep bright and positive and you will attract good will and support.

- If you can't say something good, say nothing. Would you trust someone who was a gossip?

- Become known for your reliability: use time management techniques so that you always meet your deadlines.

- Keep learning and developing work-based skills; stay at the leading edge of your profession.

- Enjoy your work. If you can't, then something needs to change.

Receive a Compliment Graciously

Someone says, 'Wow, you are looking great!' How do you respond?

Do you say:

1 Thanks.

2 I don't believe you.

3 Oh no, I'm not. I've put on tons of weight and my skin is bad and ...

When someone pays you a compliment it is most ungracious to argue with them. Good relationships are based on positive and supportive behaviour. Who will bother to compliment you again if you can't accept their positive gift? So the next time someone pays you a compliment, accept it for what it is. Just say 'Thanks' and believe it!

What Goes Around Comes Around

This is a new way of saying 'You reap what you sow'. Which is yet another way of saying that we create our own realities.

Because the quality of our relationships reflects our own personal development, we can always check our progress in this way. So reflect on your own behaviour.

- If people are showing you love you must be demonstrating it.

- If colleagues are enthusiastic about your project it's because you believe in it.

- If a partner is treating you with respect and attention it's because you feel that you deserve it.

Choose to create amazing relationships.

Focus on Your Strengths

We have a natural tendency to bring ourselves down rather than lift ourselves up. Our social conditioning has inclined us to fit in with expectations, and as we grow up we are assailed by self-doubts and self-criticisms. Negative self-beliefs create low self-esteem. There is absolutely nothing to be gained by bringing yourself down.

Lift yourself into the positive spiral of high self-esteem by focusing on your strengths. Dig deep: you have many amazing abilities that you keep forgetting about.

My strengths are:

- ....

- ....

- ....

Make a long list of all your strengths. Now live them!

Use Your Anger

When the sparks start flying we are often assailed by a confusing mixture of emotions, including, fear, resentment, guilt, excitement, hatred and violence.

Next time this happens to you, take the following steps:

- Don't be afraid of your anger; accept it and allow yourself to feel it.

- Recognise that this is your own powerful energy.

- Visualise a volcano going off inside you that fills you with energy and power.

- This initial inner (visualised) blast will clear your mind and buy you some time so that you can act and speak coherently and assertively.

Use your anger effectively and reclaim your power.

Going For It

- Write a page on why you want your specific goal.

- Make detailed notes on how your life will be when you achieve it (how fabulous you will feel, how much you deserve this, etc.). Keep this page and read it if you lose focus.

- Visualise your outcome. See your success in your mind's eye. Imagine how you will feel: feel it!

- Write your action plan. Note all the steps you will need to take and create realistic deadlines for yourself.

- Be prepared for obstacles and make contingency plans.

- Congratulate yourself as you complete each step towards your goal.

Start Buzzing With Natural Highs

Put some zap into your life by triggering your body's own natural feel-good chemicals:

Dance – get your adrenaline going and the natural amphetamine PEA will keep you energised.

Anticipate – get that adrenaline rush of anticipation.

Make Love – sex releases the high-energy hormone adrenaline, and afterwards you can relax in a flood of endorphins.

Laugh – it deepens the breath and lifts the endorphin level, which protects against negativity. Lift your energy and get out of that negative cycle and into a positive one.

Get creative and start buzzing.

Embracing Your Negativity

If you are feeling dissatisfied, unfulfilled and flat, the last thing you want to be told is that these negative feelings may have a positive aspect.

But they do.

When we can understand the concept of embracing our negativity we can make great strides in our personal development. We are members of an amazing and powerful species and we have been born in order to realise our incredible potential.

If who we are does not match who we want to be, we will be restless and unhappy with ourselves. Let your dissatisfaction show you where you need to change!

Embrace your negativity.

For Women

So often women struggle with a desire to please those around them in order to keep everyone happy.

How many men do you know who do this?

Striving for perfection leaves us unhappy, angry, unfulfilled and never satisfied. Why don't we just stop beating ourselves up?

- Learn to recognise the difference between achieving important goals and ruining your life.

- Why does your life have to stay on hold until you are the perfect weight / have the perfect qualifications / have the perfect relationship ...?

- Tune in to your feelings and you will know when you have gone too far.

Only Believe

Everything is a question of belief; you are what you think you are. A woman who knows her own worth has had to learn to let go of her negative self-beliefs in order to embrace positivity and self-esteem.

- Pay attention to your mental processes: what sort of thoughts do you have?

- Observe the ways you think about yourself and how these ways go on to affect your actions.

- Are you kind to yourself?

- Are you often fearful, or is there an inner voice that brings you hope in times of uncertainty?

Change the beliefs that aren't working for you.

Put Yourself First

You can't give if you have nothing to give. If your emotional well has run dry you need to fill it.

Women are natural nurturers: we love to take care of others and we are good at it! But often we find ourselves overstepping the line and giving so much that we have nothing left for ourselves.

Whenever:

- you feel your smile sticking to your face
- you are saying yes when you are longing to say no
- you are feeling used
- you are feeling angry with the world

it is time to put yourself first.

Hope Springs Eternal

Sometimes life really hits us between the eyes and we lose our self-confidence and self-belief. For a time the world can seem a dark and lonely place.

But we live in a constantly changing universe; we ourselves are always moving forward as we develop and grow, and there really is a light at the end of every dark tunnel.

Staying positive does not mean pretending that all is well when it obviously isn't. It means accepting your feelings (the sad as well as the glad) and knowing that you will once again feel the hope and energy that will guide you forward.

Creative Cooking

Tests show that the colour of our food can send signals to the brain that may be stronger than our sense of taste and smell.

Experts in nutrition say that eating a variety of coloured foods can make us feel more satisfied (good news for dieters).

Nutritionists suggest that colours indicate nutrients and that we will gain a greater variety of vitamins and minerals if we eat a wide selection of different coloured fruits and vegetables.

Be creative in the kitchen and eat colourful fruits and vegetables so that your meals boost your mood as well as your health.

— 12 —

Bring Your Skeletons
Out of the Closet

We have all thought and done things that we wished we hadn't. We all make mistakes sometimes.

But if you have hidden away your secret thoughts, feelings and behaviours, then you are also carrying a burden of guilt and shame, as well as the fear that they will be revealed.

Why not open those closet doors and bring out your skeletons? Try this – you have nothing to lose and everything to gain:

- Invite your skeletons out for an airing.
- Examine each one coolly.
- Remedy anything that you can.
- Let them rattle off in peace.

— 13 —

How Do You Wake Up?

Let's take an ordinary day in your life when nothing feels particularly terrible or wonderful.

- You wake up and ... How do you greet this day?
- Is this a perfect day or 24 hours of hassle?
- Is your life a precious gift or are you just struggling to survive?

Believe it or not, you can choose the quality of your experiences: it's not what happens to you that counts but rather how you deal with what happens to you.

Choose positivity every time!

How to Be Happy

We search for many things to make us happy, but we can never find happiness outside ourselves. A diamond ring, a fabulous car, even a gorgeous partner cannot create happiness and joy for us.

If you are feeling downhearted, go into the world and look for something to be glad about:

- Admire a sunset.

- Enjoy the smell of fresh mown grass.

- Feel the wind in your hair.

- Hear the laughter in the street.

- Watch the clouds scuttling across the sky.

The miracle of life is yours. Just look for beauty and you will find it everywhere.

Be Creative

Although we are all creative, most of us struggle to accept our own creativity: 'I haven't any creative skills; I can't paint, sing, draw, dance, knit, cook ...'

It's often possible to trace these negative beliefs back to our childhood (for example, a teacher telling you you were hopeless at art). Don't let a criticism from childhood wreck a lifetime of potential creativity.

- Everything you do is creative.
- You are an artist, creating your own life's work.
- You create your thoughts, your relationships, your environment.
- Let your creative juices flow.

Become a Believing Mirror

When we hit a difficult patch it's hard to find the energy to support others (we need all our strength to keep ourselves together).

But when the going is good we can give this support. Believing mirrors reflect a person's greatness, potential and positivity. Become one for someone who needs it.

Reflect this person's positive self-belief: 'You can do it', 'Give it your best shot', 'You are really doing great', 'You deserve it'. As you start to do this for others, you will find others will start to do it for you (you attract whatever you radiate). Yes, this life is truly amazing!

Stop Trying to be Perfect

- I can't get this absolutely right.
- I'm not good enough.
- It's not quite good enough.
- Nothing I ever do is just right.

Are these words familiar?

Nobody is perfect. We are always making mistakes because this is how we learn (yes, even us grown-ups).

A toddler will fall over hundreds of times before she can become an expert walker; we know she needs to practise. Now think of yourself as a grown-up toddler (which you are) and recognise that you too need to practise new skills. While practising is fine, a continual quest for perfection is not.

The Moment Is Now

Your power always lies in the moment because later never exists (it's always in the future). So be here now, feel the immediacy of your life and value it.

We so often spend time regretting the past and worrying about the future, but we only ever really have the present (the past is gone and the future is always the future).

Whenever you feel stretched today, remind yourself to stay in the present moment and you will feel calm and complete. Appreciate this precious moment of your life, it's all you ever really have!

Create Free Time

Are you busy juggling all the parts of your life in what feels like a never-ending circus performance? Do you sometimes drop the plates? Hold on a moment; put those plates down (no, the world won't stop if you do).

Do the following:

- Create lists of things that need doing.

- Refer to these lists frequently.

- Prioritise your jobs. Ruthlessly delete all those that are unnecessary.

- Stop procrastinating – it drains all self-esteem.

- Say 'no' and 'yes' when you need to.

- Feel free to have free time, and don't go filling it up with things to do!

Are You Addicted?

Addictive behaviour is compulsive because it promises to fill that gnawing empty space inside. Of course it can't ever do this.

We can be addicted to so many things: abusive relationships, overeating, undereating, drinking, drugs (illegal or prescribed), smoking, overworking, overspending, overexercising ... the list is endless.

If we are compulsively using any behaviour to hide from our true feelings and to punish ourselves, then we are addicted. Some addictions are life-threatening and others threaten the quality of our life.

If you are involved in any self-harming behaviour then you will know it.

Help is available when you are ready.

Welcome Silence

One simple way to strengthen our creative awareness is to welcome silence regularly into our lives.

Email, texting, mobile phones, car phones, TV, Internet ... we are all so busy communicating our thoughts to others. This high-velocity, high-voltage society encourages us to stay in touch with everyone except ourselves.

- Turn off all communication devices or go and find somewhere quiet and peaceful.
- Welcome silence into your life.
- Do this for a few minutes every day; make a habit of it.

Listen with your heart and stay in touch with your deepest needs.

An Oasis of Calm

Take a moment to look at your environment. Do you come home to an oasis of peace and tranquillity or do you arrive back to unfinished jobs and clutter?

If you are juggling family, career and domesticity, an oasis of calm may seem a tall order. And so it is, but you can find some small space for your personal oasis. If you aren't juggling lifestyles you may still feel that a neat and tidy home is hard to achieve. Whatever your personal situation, try bringing some good vibrations into your surroundings.

De-cluttering even a small space will create an oasis of calm.

The Real You

The real you is full of life and vitality; you are amazing, powerful and creative. But sometimes you forget who you really are.

Visualise the real you:

- Sit quietly, close your eyes, slow down your breathing and relax for a few moments.

- Now imagine that you are full of creativity and positivity.

- Feel the energy that this brings.

- See the real you in full flow and recognise who you really are.

- When you open your eyes, know that you are already on the way to making your visualisation come true.

Are You Too Nice?

Being too nice, too sweet and too pleasing can lead us into a load of trouble.

Yes, it really is quite possible to be too nice, and if you think that you have never been too saccharine sweet for your own comfort then think again.

Just how nice you are prepared to be?:

- Do you feel taken for granted?

- Are you worried about what others think?

- Do you ever think that some people are 'better' than you?

- Do you often use the word 'sorry'?

- Do you ever not say what you really mean?

Stop being a people pleaser and start pleasing yourself.

The Spirit of Christmas

Christmas is a time for forgiveness and letting go. This is the true meaning of the season. Let this Christmas become an opportunity for you to clear up any difficult relationships.

- Remember that forgiveness means letting go of old hurts.
- Look into your heart and ask yourself whom you are finding it hard to forgive.
- Imagine that this Christmas will be the last time that you ever see this person.
- What could you say or do to clear up this relationship?
- Now say or do it for real!

Open your own heart and feel the true meaning of the season.

Can't Cope?

If you have reached breaking point and you really can't cope, then slow down and take a look at where you are going (emotionally) and why.

Five ways to help you to start coping:

1 Get off your hamster wheel. If everything is just too much then you have reached emotional overload.

2 Become aware that something needs to change. Where are your emotional energy leaks?

3 Express your feelings.

4 Take action. Make any changes that you need to make.

5 Nurture yourself. Put your needs first at this time. You deserve time for yourself – make sure you get it.

Detox

According to research, five minutes of energetic skin brushing has the same effect on muscle tone as thirty minutes of jogging!

Skin brushing helps to distribute fat deposits and energises, tones and detoxifies the whole body. leaving you glowing and revitalised.

It is recommended daily before your shower. Use a natural fibre-bristle brush.

Brush on dry skin, always brushing towards the heart in long strokes.

Start on the soles of your feet and then up each leg, over the buttocks and up the lower back.

Move over the abdomen (anti-clockwise), then over the arms, neck, throat, chest (avoiding nipples), shoulders and back.

Teach Your Children Well

Our negative self-beliefs stand between us and our self-esteem, and we learned these beliefs in our childhood.

We know so much today about the power of positive thinking and the results of negative criticisms. This knowledge is invaluable, and we can use it to encourage and empower our children by supporting them in a positive and life-affirming way.

Parenting is hard, but we know how to give our children a positive start in life so that they will have respect for themselves and others.

Let us all empower our children and help to secure a generation of young people who are high in self-esteem.

Have Fun

Life can get so serious, can't it? We try so hard to achieve and make the best of ourselves that it can sometimes seem that our days have lost their sparkle.

There is one very easy way to lighten up and that is to connect with our own inner child. Yes, you really do have a child inside you! That sweet little girl / boy who loved to dress up and play imaginary games and used to dance and sing with gay abandon is still part of you.

Reconnect with that childlike spontaneous creative energy.

Let go and have some fun!

You Are a Success

This is a really uplifting tip and great fun to do with others.

Get some very large sheets of paper and lots of coloured felt tips and crayons (it's just like being back at nursery school).

Now make a Success List. This is a list of everything you are successful at or have been a success at. Go back as far as you can (learning to ride a bike, to swim, to drive ...) Make your list beautiful and colourful and stick it up on a wall where it is highly visible. Keep adding to your list and watch your achievements grow.

You see, you are a success!

Celebrate

Celebrate the fact that you have recognised your power to change an ordinary life into a great life! And know that as you improve your own life you enhance the lives of others.

And when you are feeling too low to be bothered with all these hundreds of tips and techniques, always remember that you are not alone. We are all on our own paths of self-development and sometimes the going does get tough.

Never doubt that you are progressing and know that all the love and support you need will always be with you.

With all my very best wishes and thoughts to you all.

60 Ways to Change Your Life

LYNDA FIELD

Are you stuck in a routine or feel the need to make a fresh start? Then this little book will inspire you to embrace change and face life with a positive attitude. It will help you take control of your destiny and change your life for the better – forever.

60 Ways to Feel Amazing

LYNDA FIELD

This little book is positively brimming with ways to bring positive energy into your life.

Try these simple and effective tips for your body and soul and you will discover how to feel amazing throughout the day, throughout your life.

60 Tips for Self-Esteem

Quick ways to Boost your Confidence

LYNDA FIELD

Packed with easy but highly effective tips and techniques for banishing self-doubt and boosting self-esteem, this is an essential book for those now ready to take control of their lives.

Positive self-esteem is vital for success and happiness. Anything is possible when we're feeling good about ourselves, just as everything seems beyond our reach when our confidence is low. Lynda Field's *60 Tips for Self-Esteem* shows you how it is possible to assert yourself each and every day. Positive, upbeat and full of laughter, this book will help you:

- Develop self-esteem at home and work
- Change negative self-beliefs
- Be true to yourself
- Be your own best friend

Creating Self-Esteem

A Practical Guide to Realising Your True Worth

LYNDA FIELD

When your self-esteem is high you feel great; you are creative and strong and able to embrace life's challenges. But when you are feeling low you can be held back by doubt, self-criticism and fear.

Creating Self-Esteem, from the bestselling author of *60 Ways to Feel Amazing*, is a practical and inspirational approach to developing self-awareness and confidence. Expert counsellor Lynda Field shows with warmth and humour how to balance the self at every level – the spiritual, mental, emotional and physical. You will soon discover your true worth and have the tools to realise your full potential.

60 Ways to Heal Your Life

Practical Tips for Inspiration

LYNDA FIELD

60 Ways to Heal Your Life is about knowing the person you want to be and living the life you want to live.

Building upon the wisdom of her phenomenally successful little book of *60 Ways to Feel Amazing*, Lynda Field shows you how to heal your life and look to a positive and fulfilling future. Written with humour and insight, *60 Ways to Heal Your Life* sets out the small steps that will inspire you to make quantum leaps towards improving your life. Discover how to:

- stay cool and find calm
- do whatever turns you on
- heal past hurts
- go boldly forward

More than 60 Ways to Make Your Life Amazing

A Complete Guide for Women

LYNDA FIELD

You are amazing! But right now you might be feeling a little blue, a little tired or a little fed up. The truth is you can have it all – you just need to know what you want from life and how to get it.

From the bestselling author of *60 Ways to Feel Amazing* comes this highly practical and inspirational guide for women who want to live life to the full. Whatever the issues are in your life, Lynda Field takes you straight to the heart of the problem. Through practical exercises and over 120 motivational 'power points', her upbeat guidance will help you develop a new sense of personal strength and a positive, energised approach to life, which is, after all, amazing.

The Self-Esteem Workbook

An Interactive Approach to Changing Your Life

LYNDA FIELD

Are you low in self-esteem? Do you lack self-belief? If you feel that you are under-achieving, here is your chance to boost your Feel-Good Factor. Learn to believe in yourself and make your life happy and successful!

- Improve your personal relationships

- Enhance your health and prosperity

- Communicate your needs clearly

- Identify your best career and vocation

- Trust yourself and your intuition

- Develop your spirituality

The Self-Esteem Workbook is packed with practical and effective techniques and exercises which will help you to bring a new sense of creativity and vision to your life. Reassuring and simple, this book shows you how to develop and put into practice a self-esteem action plan to meet your your own specific needs.

Just Do It Now!

How to Become the Person You Most Want to Be

LYNDA FIELD

You can become the person you most want to be. This uplifting and inspiring book is a step-by-step guide to the simple principles which lie behind the truth that we create our own reality.

But more than that, it also shows you how to overcome a natural fear of change so that you can make your vision of who you are match your vision of who you want to be. In this way you can learn how to harness every aspect of yourself (mind, body, spirit and emotions) to the task of bringing motivation and enthusiasm into all areas of your life.

Bestselling author Lynda Field offers original exercises, practical tips and techniques which she has specially designed for your unique and specific needs. 'You are a powerhouse of amazing energy' she says. 'You can decide to make the most of your life: Just Do It *Now*.'

60 Ways to Change Your Life	£2.50
60 Ways to Feel Amazing	£2.50
The Little Book of Woman Power	£2.50
60 Tips for Self-Esteem	£6.99
Creating Self-Esteem	£6.99
60 Ways to Heal Your Life	£6.99
More Than 60 Ways to Make Your Life Amazing	£6.99
Self-Esteem for Women	£7.99
The Self-Esteem Workbook	£10.99
Just Do It Now!	£6.99

ALL VERMILION BOOKS ARE AVAILABLE THROUGH MAIL ORDER OR FROM YOUR LOCAL BOOKSHOP.

PAYMENT MAY BE MADE USING ACCESS, VISA, MASTERCARD, DINERS CLUB, SWITCH AND AMEX, OR CHEQUE, EUROCHEQUE AND POSTAL ORDER (STERLING ONLY).

EXPIRY DATE .... SWITCH ISSUE NO.

SIGNATURE ....

PLEASE ALLOW £2.50 FOR POST AND PACKING FOR THE FIRST BOOK AND £1.00 PER BOOK THEREAFTER.

ORDER TOTAL: £................................. (INCLUDING P&P)

ALL ORDERS TO:
VERMILION BOOKS, BOOKS BY POST, TBS LIMITED, THE BOOK SERVICE, COLCHESTER ROAD, FRATING GREEN, COLCHESTER, ESSEX, CO7 7 DW, UK.

TELEPHONE: (01206) 256 000   FAX: (01206) 255 914

NAME ....

ADDRESS...

....

Please allow 28 days for delivery. Please tick box if you do not wish to receive any additional information. □
Prices and availability subject to change without notice.